A Council

Kids can be horrible, I was no exception .... ___
2022.

Is there anything like it anymore? Will there ever be anything like it Fagain? Somehow I don't think so.
I am a Council Estate Creation,(Cec) a breed born out of a way of life that simply doesn't exist today. Of course we can all relive our childhood memories, our childhood fears, hopes, aspirations, but all with the distortion of youth and an ignorance of the grown ups world, so I am not claiming that mine was anything different or anything special. Looking back I can say that life lived on a Council Estate in the 50's and 60's where everybody knew everybody else and no-one sought to be any better than anyone else is something that until you lose you can never fully appreciate.
I am a Council Estate Creation (Cec) and along with others who were created with me I want to share our stories with you.

Let me take you to a Council Estate in Reading, Berkshire, all you have to do is wear a woollen jumper with holes in the elbows, put different coloured socks on your dirty feet, pull up your short grey trousers or black plain skirt and put chewing gum in your pocket with your catapult or pink hankie and come with me.

*

Mary, Mungo and Midge.

Kim, for some reason my mum had christened me Kim. Legend has it that Bob (my elder brother) was sent out into the big wide world to find a name for me and came back with this one !!!
Whether he was influenced by a fan of Rudyard Kipling or he was just jealous that being small I was getting all the attention, we will never know, after all he had been the cream on the milk for mum and dad for four years until I came along !!
'Hi, what's your name?' 'Kim' 'Tim?' no Kim, 'Jim?' no Kim, 'Kim that's a girl's name' 'Did I say Kim?' I meant Alan'..and so it went on.
So let's paint the picture, a darker skinned boy (My name is Sue, how do you do?) called Kim, did I suffer any inappropriate teasing from my fellow Cecs? No, not especially, we all took the mickey out of each other all the time, that's what we did, I was one of them and happy to be so..I was a Council Estate Creation and proud of it.
Our house was an end house, exactly the same as all the others but on the end of a row, which was good because we had a bigger garden, so I suppose it

wasn't really exactly the same as the others. We had a coal shed opposite the back door so getting in the coal was easy using the scuttle, so easy in fact that us kids used to do it. On very cold mornings having scraped the ice off the inside of as many windows as we could dad would clear the grate of the previous day's fire and prepare it for relighting.

With a layer of coal resting on rolls of tightly twisted together pages of the Daily Mirror dad would light an edge of said pages and we'd all stand back rubbing our hands together pretending it was getting warmer. If the flames were slow to fully ignite dad would hold a full page of the tabloid against the mouth of the fire, covering it completely and we'd listen to the rush of air being sucked up the chimney. Using this method one of two things would inevitably happen, either after just a few minutes the fire would become a blazing inferno, or the page held over it would burst into flames and we'd all spend the next twenty minutes coughing our heads off, or of course, both.

The back garden was dad's vegetable plot (well a quarter of it was, the rest was just long grass and dandelions). Every Sunday morning he would dig his little veg bit over ready for his 'taters, cabbages, and onions. This Sunday morning would be no different to any other Sunday morning.

Having checked his watch (nearly opening time) he kicked his muddy wellies against the coal shed wall to de-mud them, pulled them off and made his way into the kitchen in stockinged feet to get ready for the pub. His weekly obligations were completed, his mind guilt free.

At the sink he filled the washing-up bowl with soapy water and by cupping said soapy water in his hands and then throwing it into his face making sloshing and gurgling noises, had his idea of a wash. After that he would change into his better clothes and disappear out the back door towards the Happy Prospect pub in Coronation Square or the George and Dragon on the Bath Road, in a cloud of Brylcreem and Golden Virginia fumes.

*

Rag Tag and Bobtail

We had a big front room (which posh people referred to as a lounge, living room, or sitting room)

Our 'front room' was dominated by a huge television with a tiny screen held up by four skinny legs. Like the sun, everything in the room revolved around the television. The sofa, the chairs, the coffee table with the view of the Rialto Bridge under glass on it, even Pele the budgie in his wire cage.

Three channels were available on our black and white television as on all televisions in those days and programmes ended before midnight when they were turned off to the sound of the National Anthem and the sight of a little white silvery dot disappearing into the centre of its screen. For extra entertainment value and physical exercise to select a channel or turn the television off and on you had to get up from your comfy seat and 'turn the telly over' by turning a big round button on the front of it. Sometimes for reasons better known to itself the 'picture' would start to rapidly disappear up or down into its own little box like a hamster on its wheel. When it occurred (which was too often) the horizontal hold button had to be tweaked until the hamster fell off and the picture slowed and eventually righted itself.

There was also a Vertical Hold Button but as far as I was concerned that was just for keeping the horizontal hold button company.

Oh, did I mention that once the television's on button switch was turned on you had to wait for the 'set' to warm up. Well, once the televisions on button was turned on you had to wait for the 'set' to warm up. Television, it was never going to catch on, too expensive and too much trouble.

*

It was my sister Sandra's idea, or was it Serena's not sure, it certainly wasn't mine or my brother Bob's, although for some reason he always got a share of the spoils.

We stood a few feet apart from each other, me (Sandra or Serena depending on who lost the toss) and in an acutely embarrassing coy manner skipped towards each other singing 'I'm a little Dutch Boy' flapping our arms against our sides like stunted, demented penguins. When we met in the middle we circled each other and skipped back to start all over again.

Our adult audience, having recently left the pub with our parents to come to our house for more bevvies, clapped and tried their best not to laugh, yawn, or excuse themselves to go for a long overdue wee. After 5 or 10 minutes of this torture (for me and the audience, I'm sure my female siblings quite enjoyed it) money was given to us by the said audience for either amusing them or getting us to (please) stop. We soon realised that for variety (you have to keep your fans wanting) we rehearsed little plays and performed them for everyone's delectation…and this proved more profitable..so 'Footsteps' and other plays written by me became the first time I ever exposed myself to an adoring public.

*

Secret Squirrel

'How long can you hold this cactus in one hand?'

'How long can you leave this cold bottle of milk on your bare belly?'

'How far can you walk balancing a phone book on your head?'

'How many steps can you go doing the crab?'

'How long can you stand on your head?'

'How many steps could you jump over, holding onto the bannister and leaping from the top of the stairs to the bottom?'

How long could you hold your head down in the washing up bowl full of cold water without drowning?

These and other 'dares' we challenged each other when there was nothing on the telly and mum and dad were down the pub and it was too dark to go out (and nobody had invented playstations and the like yet). Monopoly, Cluedo, Risk, Escalado, Ludo, Game of Life, Draughts, Twister, Mouse Trap, Operation, Trouble, Stratego and many more comfortable games were mostly available but we could play them anytime, with no adults around it was time to just be profoundly silly, and possibly get killed.

Blindfolded and sat on a chair in the middle of the front room we all took it in turn to be choked, gagged, made sick or simply poisoned. A portion of edible or not so edible foodstuff (when I say foodstuff I mean anything that could be put in the mouth and mastigated, swallowed or spat out).

Teaspoons containing vinegar, mustard, ketchup, chopped apple, oxo cube, onion, porridge oats, lemon, syrup, tomato, piccalilli, coffee, tea, jelly cubes, drinking chocolate and anything else we could find.

If it wouldn't fit on a teaspoon, it was fed by hand and forcibly pushed home.

Now you might think you could easily tell what was being put in your mouth...try it when your nose is pinched tightly together with one, or for good measure two, of your mum's vice like wooden clothes pegs. Your sense of taste completely deserts you, please trust someone who has had experience of such lunacy!

*

Roger Ramjet

'Tuberculosis' Mrs Bell said' That's what your mum has, that's why you are staying here with us for a few weeks while she's in hospital'

I didn't know what Tuberculosis was but it sounded horrible so I didn't want to know.

'Your dad cannot cope with you all so you are being fostered out with us Kimmy.

'Why can't I be fostered out with my brother and sister?'

I asked Mrs Bell.

'They are together over the other side of the Southcote Estate' I added, as if she didn't know.

'Because you are always fighting Kimmy' said Mrs Bell.

I looked over at the table by my new bed and the pile of comics and tray with biscuits and a glass of milk on.

'Oh, ok' I said.

'Your dad's coming over Thursday Kimmy, ' she said. But I didn't hear her.

*

Weymouth is a long way from Reading, the other side of the planet in fact and where my auntie Dot lived. I remember dad saying 'You'll know when you reach Weymouth because the train doesn't go any further or it will go into the sea and besides I've asked the guard to keep an eye out for you. I didn't know what Auntie Dot looked like but Dad said she knew what I looked like as he hurried me onto the train and handed me my single suitcase and a greaseproof bag.

It would take hours to get there apparently so I had to sit down patiently and not make a nuisance of myself. I sat alone looking out of the window while it got darker and the train got slower, sometimes looking down at the rails hoping they weren't under water and had seaweed stuck to them.

I had sandwiches in the greaseproof bag and my latest copy of the Beano and I ignored them and the train just kept on moving.

'It's for your summer holiday' mum had told me but I got the feeling it was for dad's summer holiday really. Bob (my elder brother) is already there and he said it's great,' said mum. Sandra, my younger sister was with Auntie Pusey up Southamton Street, Reading, she must have been having her own summer holiday there.

And the train kept moving.

It was no good looking out of the windows now because all I could see was my own reflection unless I shadowed my eyes with my hands and then I only saw the occasional light and huge black trees creeping along in the night.

And the train kept moving.

We were going to reach the edge of the earth and fall off it.

I took my sandwiches out of the bag and then put them back. I looked briefly at my Beano but not even the likes of Minnie the Minx, Biffo the Bear, or Roger the Dodger could ease my terrible feeling of doom. The train was still moving and it became more and more obvious to me that I was indeed destined for a watery death.

And then I heard a voice, the first one I'd heard for what seemed like an age.

'Come on lad, the next one and the last one is Weymouth'

The guard stood beside my seat, his voice coming from somewhere hidden inside a dense beard.

I sat up, my spirits lifting as the train was suddenly lit up by outside street lamps as it made its way to Weymouth Station, (in those days the train actually did go along the towns roads) Mum told me this before I left Reading but I thought she was just trying to give me something to occupy my mind during the hellish long and lonely journey.

I was looking down on the roofs of cars and aware of pedestrians moving aside as the huge smoking locomotive crawled along to its final destination and my Auntie Dot hopefully standing on the platform waiting for me.

The train shuddered to a stop, the guard threw open a door, I stepped out onto a platform blanketed in smoke and swirling dust and Auntie Dot's voice met my ears from somewhere down the platform…

'You're late'

Formidable, that's what I would have called Auntie Dot if I knew what formidable meant when I was that age. Uncle Fred was my saviour and possibly the only person who stood up to Auntie Dot although I could barely understand his heavy St. Helenian accent coupled with a slight lisp. 'He would slay 'Leave thla lad alone Dloth, heesh shly and a long waysh from home' and Auntie Dot would leave me alone until Uncle Fred was back in the backroom alone and watching his beloved cweecket, eh? cricket.

Their son was the same age as me and I could not bear him, a spoiled mummy's boy and with my big brothers help the source of all the friction that prevailed in Short Street sunny Weymouth.

Bob (bless him) would fan the flames between my cousin and I and sit back and watch the eruptions until my cousin would run crying to mummy who would then decide it was time to bathe and scrub me in the big white china kitchen sink.

On the rare occasions that we all three were on speaking terms we would go to the huge swannery and upset the equilibrium of the many swans instead. At night after my kitchen sink scrub and a bit of telly it was off to a bedroom that contained the only items that made my stay in Weymouth almost bearable, my cousin's pile of comics, five foot high and leaning against the wall. The Beano, The Dandy, The Victor, Valiant, Lion,The Hotspur,The Topper,The Beezer, Buster, Eagle, Superman, Batman, Spiderman, Daredevil, Green Lantern, The Sparky, Whizzer and Chips, and many more, I think Auntie Dot was so afraid of failing her precious son and missing a comic for him she bought them all!!

On the final day of my torment at the hands of the formidable Auntie Dot and her budding psychopath of a son we attended a huge firework display on the beach. I remember looking up at the rockets and being jolted out of my skin by the echoing bangs they produced as they flew out and over the sea and exploded.

It was a strangely moving event for me and as we walked back to Castle Dot, where our suitcases were awaiting us, somewhere loud speakers were filling the smoky air with 'The Carnival is Over' by The Seekers and I was gazing at the stars twinkling in the black sea through blurred eyes.

Maybe after all I missed something about me and my brothers holiday in Weymouth, maybe I misjudged Auntie Dot and my irksome cousin, well maybe, after all I never really wanted to be there if truth be told.

Such are nicknames.

I'd been home only a few hours and a chat with my old schoolmate Tin'ead was well overdue, lots to tell him about Weymouth.

'Mum, just popping up the road to chat to Tin'ead'

'Who?'

'Tin'ead, lives next door to the 'Little's'

Mum's face went from blank to pained in a second.

'Oh, you mean Mrs Townsend eldest David'

That was two things I didn't know about Tin'ead, one was his real name was David Townsend and the second thing, he was dead.

RIP David.

*

Hectors House

Every house on the Southcote Estate had a brick coal shed built onto the back of it and our house was no exception. Useful for storing half empty paint cans, bikes, bits of furniture, a mangle (every home should have one) and anything else that would fit in it. Sometimes even coal. I found it very handy for putting my tortoises in for their hibernation every winter. A wooden box filled with dry hay, a piece of paper with 'My name is Stubby and this is where I sleep, do not disturb' written on it with thick black felt tip and it was *'Goodnight mate see you in about three months'*

But another, far more fun use of the coal shed was for jumping off of.
At least 8ft high it was the equivalent of 16ft to us small Cecs but we needed a step up to get onto its corrugated roof, so we made use of the fence and concrete post that was attached to it. With one foot on the top of the post and fingers curled around the crumbling metal of the shed's gutter we pulled ourselves up.

An incentive not to fall was that we had to lean over my mum's fearsome looking rhubarb plant that was always trying to snatch at our legs with its trifid like tentacles. It was a monstrous plant but somehow completely different when deleafed, detached and delivered to the kitchen table after sausage and mash and covered with crumble and sweet custard.

We would take it in turns each with our own unique scream as we flew through the air, Barry, his brother Malcolm, Neil, Mark, Les, Steve and me, my sisters and their friends sitting on the grass doing girly things with wool and occasionally giving us contemptuous glances. We hadn't really noticed the washing line before because the mere act of just jumping off the roof and landing back on earth without breaking a bone required most of our concentration and a certain level of blind stupidity. The said washing line that ran parallel to the side of the shed's roof opened up a whole new world of idiocy to us. From now on it wasn't enough to just jump off the roof (any one of the girls could do that !) Now you had to jump off the roof and over the washing line that was a good 3ft away making the jump twice as hard and three times more death defying.
If I hadn't suggested it I would not necessarily have had to attempt it first.
I did and it hurt.

With a couple of steps backwards to speed up my running take off and with my attention fixed completely on the yellow plastic washing line I hurled myself high into the air. With inches to spare I cleared the line and 8 feet up but quickly descending I had no time to prepare myself for a landing back on planet earth, a landing that would be akin to a 747 hitting the tarmac at London Heathrow. My whole body jerked as I finally hit the grass with a sickening thud. The pain radiated from the bottom of my feet up through my calves, pausing at my groin where it lingered to seize my testicles in a vice like grip, then moved up my lower back, rattled my rib cage and threatened to dislocate my arms from my shoulders, it forced my teeth into my tongue and rolled my eyes like fruit machine reels in my head.

I stood dizzy and disoriented, nevertheless, the hero, I looked quickly across at the girls to assure myself that they had seen me, they had, the world for now was mine but better still Neil was next for the jump. Not known for his athleticism more for his unathleticism Neil made his way up to the roof looking like a boy having just been ordered by his parents to get his short back and sides at the Coronation Square barbers (it mattered not what you asked for you got the same short back and sides and sharp little nips on your ears).

Having reached the coal shed roof Neil immediately closed his eyes, ran, and launched himself into the air.

I must have closed mine as well because the next thing I remember was the earth below me shuddering and a stunted Neil sounding grunt, reaching my ears. Neil had made it unscathed, when I say unscathed I do not take into account the nightmares he told me he'd had for nights after.

Steve was up next (or Spanner Legs) as he was affectionately known due to his resemblance to the tool, with bowlegs the shape and design of 3.5mm spanner.

The consensus was that given the weight of Spanner Legs and his lack of body, soaring over the washing line having left the roof behind would be a cinch for him, it wasn't.

Maybe it was his own assumption that for him it would be a breeze but his lack of judgement proved to be his downfall, if you'll excuse the fully intended pun. The majority of his body cleared the washing line his trailing left foot did not. Until the washing line had used up all its slack and tightened all was fine and dandy, then when it had reached its elastic limit and mum's clothes prop snapped in half things took a downhill turn (if you forgive another attempt at a dreadful pun). Poor old Spanner Legs was literally catapulted to the ground at great speed (probably faster than the ambulance that took him to The Battle

Hospital, Oxford Road Reading with a broken ankle and sprained wrist. Still things could have been worse, he could have landed on me!

*

H.R. Pufnstuf
'What else did you get for Christmas?' Was the question (always asked with a mixture of sarcasm and jealousy) that greeted any kid seen riding a new bike or scooting a new scooter along the streets of the estate. I only got to hear it once though. I was given a nice shiny bike for Christmas. I had it for a whole two weeks before my dear dad sold it for either the rent, beer or betting money. Life had its ups and downs on a council estate.
But with that one out of the way, Christmas was on the whole a good time for us Cecs. A stocking on the bed to wake up to, (no later than 05.30 am) which was usually stuffed with chocolates (Selection box) and strangely enough because we never ate them at any other time of the year a satsuma or a tangerine (I could never identify one from the other).
For breakfast it was a squabble to see who got the 'Frosties' from the Variety Pack and who ended up with the Cornflakes. (Who wanted Cornflakes when that's what you normally had for breakfast every day of the week?) Time to be let loose on our presents, usually one that we had previously asked for and a

compendium of games that no-one had asked for (if it could be found in one of the many catalogues that littered the house, probably by the pile of Green Shield Stamps books)..a saying of the day (thanks Christine)..'*If your shoes squeaked they were on the never, never).*

Sunday Night at the London Palladium, with Bruce Forsyth (beating the clock) inspired me for one of my favourite Christmas presents of my youth. To 'Beat the Clock' the contestants were brought onto the stage and given infantile games to do against the clock with dear old Brucie diving between them attempting to make them look even sillier and awkward than they really were.

One game that caught my eye involved a gun, well more like a rifle really. It consisted of a long transparent plastic tube full of ping pong balls that were forcibly ejected when the (rifle was pumped back and forth by the rifler). The contestants were to shoot the ping pong balls at a target at least fifteen feet away scoring depending on which numbered bell they managed to hit. The little balls could travel quite a distance. The 'rifle' looked fun, I wanted one.

I don't know how mum managed it but I got my wish and on this particular Christmas morning all I had to do was take my (rifle) out of its box, assemble it and fill it with ping pong balls

Having done that I immediately aimed my new weapon at one of my sisters faces (I couldn't imagine a better way to gauge the rifles potential) and with all my strength pumped. The ping pong ball first in line crawled up the transparent tube, sat for a while at the elastic rubber bit stretched over the barrel's end, travelled two inches through the air and plopped to the carpet six inches from my feet, the second ping pong ball copied the first as did all the others.

My disappointment was overwhelming and it was obvious to me that the rifles (and their effects) on Sunday Night at the London Palladium were just camera tricks and a big con.

I was upstairs in our bedroom when Tom Brown's (you will hear more of the heroic Tom Brown later in this tome) voice echoed up the stairwell.

'Kim come down here you daft bugger'

As I walked through the doorway of the front room what felt like a thousand ping pong balls assailed my body, hitting my bare arms and bouncing off my head.

Tom Brown laughed and handed me my now ping pongballess rifle.

'See that rubber bit on the end of the barrel, you put it on the wrong way round' he said between sanctimonious chortles.

'I knew that' I said 'I was just coming downstairs to fix it'

*

Sesame Street

The Cinema was a treat for us Cec's, 'We come along on Saturday mornings treating everybody with a smile' and all that. One of us would pay the 4d to get in and make his way straight to the back doors and let in the rest of us (who had been waiting not so patiently in the rear car park). Hubbly Jubblies, Choc Ices, Popcorn, Black Jacks, Love Hearts, Sherbert Fountains and Ice cream in tubs with a little wooden spoon were consumed in great quantities whilst Lassie found the little girl stuck down the abandoned mine and Champion the Wonder Horse kicked his hooves in the air and did champion things amongst the cowboys who all wore waistcoats and spurs. Every now and again Norman Wisdom hit the big screen and his films were unmissable amongst us Cec's, they were revered. On the Beat, The Square Peg, The Early Bird, A Stitch in Time, Trouble in Store, Press for Time, Up in the World, The Bulldog Breed, Follow a Star, to name far too many, so dated now, but then again so is innocence.

*

The streets were littered with strange rounded objects that had a curious potato-like feel about them, thin leathery skin on the outside and soft pulpy yellowy flesh on the inside. The thin leathery skin was covered with small round deep indentations all of the same circular size and depth. Some were crushed under foot looking for all the world like mashed potatoes, some were still intact and looking like potatoes with holes all over them. They were in fact potatoes with holes all over them, the remnants of ammunition for our spud guns.

Every boy and many girls were the owners of a spud gun and the tiny red weals they caused on the skin when shot at and hit by them. The barrel was pushed back into the body of the gun, then the small protruding nozzle at the other end of the barrel pushed into the potato where it was forcibly clogged by a pellet shaped potato bullet.

The gun was then pointed towards the nearest available expanse of bare flesh and fired.

The recipient of the pellet shaped clog of potato gave out an 'ouch' sound and swore, then the whole procedure was repeated again by the said recipient with only vengeance in mind.

Pea guns were very popular with us Cecs and the local grocer's trade in boxed dried peas must have gone through the roof!

They were spring loaded plastic guns and held quite a few dried peas in their magazines' 'High Noon' and

'Gunfight at the OK Corral' were played out amongst us Cecs on an almost daily basis.

Some of the tougher and more enterprising Cecs amongst us strived to acquire Gnat guns, (air pistols) these were more spiteful weapons and made of metal and firing lead pellets a preference for the budding villains amongst us. Barry and I devised our own weapon of course, one that could almost be safe for indoor use.

We *borrowed* his mum's dressmaking pins, cut up tiny lengths of wool and with an acquired dexterity tied the wool with cotton wool tightly under the head of the pins and fluffed them up with our fingers. Placing our handmade 'darts' point first into the end of a drinking straw (the plastic ones were far better than paper ones that usually ended up a soggy mess having been layered with a copious amount of spit) we were armed with our own monkey killing blow pipes, albeit not having any monkeys to kill.

Accuracy was the key word here, with careful aiming and the right amount of forced blow we could get our pin dart to stick into the King of Hearts head from a selection of playing cards leaning against the bedroom wall a yard away.

*

How?

It was a Grundig, all things that had the name Grundig on them were the 'bees knees' to us Cecs. It was a large stereogram with twin speakers, built in radio and a compartment to store L.P,s (long playing vinyl records usually with 6 tracks on either side) E.P.s (extended playing records with usually 3 tracks on either side) or singles...it had a mechanism to enable it to play records one after the other and a green strip that magically elongated when the sound was turned up. Dad told me that if ever the green strip reached the far end of its little slotted window the stereogram would 'blow up'. Ours gave off a certain warm smell to me that told me this was important and 'blowing up' a real incentive to keep the volume down. Nice one dad!.

When records were played on this contraption it was always when at least one parent was around and usually at parties or adults get togethers.

When no parents or other adults were around it was a totally different story. It wasn't the contraptions' ability to play records and therefore produce music that attracted us, it was its amazing lid that entertained. Made of solid wood and extremely heavy to smaller fingers it had a spring like action when closed. It would travel quite happily on its own under the force of gravity but just as it was to settle into the closed position it would do a little bounce, pause and then drop the last inch or so slowly and under mechanical control.

After a few test drops and successful landings of said lid, the game of 'chicken' was the obvious schoolboy extension.

Barry would go first as it was his idea, he would do the putting, I would do the closing. Barry would put the fingers of both hands on the edge under the lid and I would gently start the lid on its way down. With eyes tightly closed and his body braced for the pain that was sure to be his and his alone the lid came down at a speed. Less than half an inch from the skin on his chubby knuckles the lid did its little trick, it ceased its falling, it stopped, paused and with the kiss of an angel on his fingers came to rest.

'Phew' he exclaimed as he retrieved his hand 'That sure was scary'

We did it a few times more, taking it in turns until it all got a bit boring.

'How can we liven it up?' I said to Barry and we stared at each other until I saw a wide smile grow on his face. 'I know a way," he replied. 'Let's play a new game, I've just thought of called 'Beat the Lid' and I pretended with all my might that I didn't see his hands go to the front of his trousers. The next thing I saw but didn't want to see was my best friend with his willy exposed. I watched transfixed as he stood by the side of the Grundig and took up the classic weeing in the bush by the side of the road stance.

'You are kidding?' I said looking at the T.V. that wasn't switched on.

`Go on, I'm ready!' He said, placing his little pink member on the edge of what was now the Grundigs huge open mouth. 'Close the lid down, quick'

I gave the lid a gentle nudge and although I tried to look away I found it impossible. The lid came down very fast in slow motion and I was convinced that at any second Barry was going to jerk back, laugh and put his willy back where it belonged, but he didn't.

As the would-be wooden guillotine descended he gave out a prolonged scream that culminated in 'Oh my God, Jesus Christ' took a deep breath exhaled and fell to his knees taking his willy with him. The lid carried on its pausing and bouncing back routine and then gently closed with the most satisfying, mechanical sigh.

'Your go' Barry said looking up at me from the carpet 'Or are you Chicken ?'

I must have done it, maybe the fear I felt at the time eradicated all memory of it, but I went on to father three beautiful children so I must have 'Beat the lid'. One go each and we went back to playing cards, 'Beat the Lid' was definitely a one off and we were both secretly glad that it was.

*

Flipper

As a family we never owned a car so holidays were always either by train or coach and we always went to one of three locations… St.Tropez, Monaco and Cannes…were on different planets as far as we were concerned so it was either Littlehampton, Hayling Island or Butlins at Bognor Regis.

A shilling for the first one to see the sea mum would say and then she'd give us each a little wage packet size envelope with our holiday money, a florin or if we were very lucky a half a crown in it. We'd stay in a caravan or mobile home and spend most of our time on the beach eating sandy sandwiches and groping through rock pools for crabs and other little nasties.

I remember it as if it were just yesterday, we'd just arrived at the 'Ponderosa' a campsite in Hayling Island when I heard my friend Les was staying in a caravan not far from ours. We'd take it in turns to have wild parties while our parents were spending every night at the 'entertainments' We'd play Monopoly, drink bottle after bottle of Corona Ice Cream Soda and eat far too many crisps and chocolate bars.

Les couldn't swim, he told me, so one night we decided to go out for a 'midnight swim' and I would teach him.

At eight o'clock midnight we stole away from our caravans and siblings and under the cover of darkness made our way out of the site to the beach. Illuminated by a huge silvery white moon in a cloudless sky and the coloured lights from the promenade the sea looked nothing like it did in the daylight. It had a flat and almost waveless lead hued surface with white foam left clinging to the sand as it gently changed its mind and receded. When it rolled back in it had ice cold fingers that caressed our naked feet and sent shivers up and down our bare legs.

'I will learn to swim tomorrow, ' Les said as I grabbed his arm and tugged him further in, ' Come on we'll get used to it' I shivered back'.

We paddled for what seemed like an age, the reflection from the promenade growing duller and the light from the moon, now with no competition growing brighter.

As we paddled further out we felt the water was actually getting shallower and in some places there were sand banks and no water at all. After a while there didn't appear to be enough water to swim in and our short trousers remained dry no matter how far out we went.

Then just as we were on the cusp of turning back for a packet of crisps, a drink of Corona and another game of Monopoly in our warm, cosy caravan I felt the tentacles of icy water lapping against my testacles.

We'd made it, I felt sure we were halfway to Africa because that's where all the oceans went, to Africa, and so elated was I that I dived forward and immediately died of cold. I didn't really but if dying of cold felt like that then I died of cold. I stood erect in the water (no innuendo intended) swaying, rubbing my eyes with the backs of both hands and spitting salty water back where it belonged.

'Your turn Les' I hoped I said through chattering teeth, but Les wasn't listening he was bent over, hands on knees staring intently at the water, or to be more precise something under the water.

Crabs, little white crabs, thousands and thousands of them scrabbling about on the sea bed, encircling our feet and clearly very angry at our intrusions.

Swimming instructions from me were completely dismissed, our only aim was to get to the shore line, out of the water and away from these marauding flesh eating crustaceans as soon as possible. Taking high leaping, loping steps, our knees going higher than our heads we splashed our awkward way back to the welcoming glow of the promenade lights, flicking into the cold night air, the little clinging bastards from our bare toes as we did so.

It was back a.s.a.p. to the safety of the caravan and Old Kent Road for us intrepid would-be ocean swimmers.

*

There were the big flats and the little flats, the little flats we called maisonettes, the big flats we called big flats. Situated on Granville Road opposite Prospect park they were in a row and approached by little service roads. We weren't allowed in any of them but that never stopped us. From carol singing to halloween, to collecting money for Guy Fawkes night we entered them, much to the chagrin of most of the residents who were elderly and for some reason scared to death when we appeared at their doorways dressed in halloween garb with bloodied faces.

Before I talk about the experiment* I want to talk to you about the ghost. Where you were least likely to see a ghost, I saw one, felt one, heard one, ran from one.

The big flats had lifts the maisonettes stairs, stairs that went down one flight and then turned ninety degrees to another flight. Each flight of stairs had its own lights that could be switched on as and when needed. I was a young Cec paper round boy, I had no need of lights, even if it was on the shadowy side. I was at the bottom of the last flight when something made me pause and look up from whence I'd just come down.

The figure was there and then it wasn't, it disappeared from my sight as quickly as it had appeared, behind the wall at the top of the descending stairs. I stood in shook and listened for its retreating footsteps in the fully enclosed stairwell, nothing not a sound. I had two choices to run back up the stairs and seek out what had scared me half to death or turn and run quickly out of the maisonettes doors.

It was a little drizzly but lucky for me it was not quite raining and looking back from a comfortable distance I saw nothing but a vague figure etched on my retinas.

*'The experiment'? I was hoping I would hear you say that.

Well, Barry and I had read somewhere that the diameter of a large chicken egg is about 1.75" and the typical shell thickness is 0.023"

Thus, the cross-sectional area of the shell wall is approx. ⅛ sq inch or 8 x 10~5- inch M2 which when combined with the ultimate strength, theoretically will support a 1.4x10 N load (3,000 lbs) but I'm sure you all knew that, Barry and I did.

Well I am just sure you all know that if you put an egg long-ways between your palms and press them together you will find it impossible to break the egg no matter how much pressure you are able to apply.

The fun bit of course is when the egg slips from being end on end in your grasp and it implodes and shower's you with gooey yellow egg snot.

So, to get back to our 'experiment'

We borrowed three eggs from Barry's mum's larder and took them to the seventh floor(the top) of the big flats, being careful not to be seen.

At the top we walked to the edge of the landing and looked over the side.

We were high and mighty and apart from a few parked cars safe to carry out our experiment.

Barry took hold of the first egg and holding it as if to encourage it to spin top over bottom he gently lobbed it in a high wide arc out into the nothing filled air. The egg rose gracefully and then started its inevitable descent according to as legend would have it Isaac Newton's gravitational theory.

We stood in awe watching the eggs progress down to the hard concrete surface of the big flats service road where to our utter dismay it splattered into a bright yellow raw omelette.

The second egg fared no better, even if my miss calculated lob sent it plummeting onto the grass verge and not the road resulting therefore in no visible omelette this time.

In school later, Malcolm stared at us, opened mouthed, Carol giggled and called us idiots, Mr. Palmer the science teaching looked at us and slowly nodded and said 'Well I suppose it could have occurred'

'It did' shouted Barry, 'It did' shouted me.

And it did, the third egg flew through the air, landed straight on the hard concrete of the road and bounced a good 30ft in the air before becoming our third omelette, QED.

*

Rin Tin Tin

On hot sunny days the meandering tree lined lanes of Burghfield Common called to us, the heavy scent of the wild flowers filled our nostrils, the vast rolling countryside with its promise of unbridled freedom to roam unimpeded played heavily on our senses. The want of life's unseen but awaiting adventures to be had overwhelmed our very beings is a poetic way of saying sometimes we got bored with concrete roads and skipping ropes.

Time to head off into the wilderness, which as I say is Burghfield Common, my brother Bob, sisters Sandra and Serena and the goosegog in the crumble, Barry. It doesn't take long to walk from the mess that is the Council Estate to the far less of a mess that is Burghfield Common and it is well worth the effort. And on this particular day we were all in high spirits sharing our Gobstoppers, Jelly Beans, Sherbert Lemons and Pineapple Cubes plus taking in turns swigging from a Corona bottle of Cream Soda, the latter being carefully distributed because if we were cut off from civilisation we'd need something to drink when we ate each other.

I don't remember who found the bright orange nylon rope but I do remember where it was lying, on the grass on the banks of the narrow lane on a tight corner. I don't remember whose idea it was to tie my sister Sandra up with said rope and I don't remember whose idea it was for us all to leave her lying in the middle of the lane all trussed up and unable to free herself, but we did and it was great fun.

'Don't worry Sandra we'll be back sometime tonight and untie you if there's nothing worth watching on the telly'

I don't remember who decided that enough was enough and suggested that we ought to turn back as we could no longer see her due to the high bushes and the bend in the lane, the 'joke' having run its course we started back.

I do remember helping to untie her, throwing away the nylon rope and her getting up just seconds before the milk tanker came hurtling around the corner, its air horns blasting away. I remember thinking 'Blimey' she could have been killed because the driver had no way of seeing her through all the trees and bushes as he hurtled round the bend. I do remember thinking if Sandra got all squashed I would blame Bob, him being the eldest and all.

*

Animal Magic

Mortimer Common on a blisteringly hot day, Steve, Barry, Malcolm Buzzy, Les and me armed with a copy of 'I Spy-British Wild Birds, notebooks, biros a pair of ancient binoculars bought in a junk shop and a bag containing our survival kit, Mars Bars, Crunchies, Marathons and an almost empty bottle of Corona fizzy orange without any fizz. Having identified a number of birds and argued heatedly about the identity of a few more (what the hell would an albatross be doing this far from the sea Barry it's a guillemot) we wandered down one country lane after another.

'Let's have a swig of orange' It was Barry talking to Steve who was carrying our survival kit as it was his turn to carry it. Come to think of it, it was always Steve's turn to carry the 'survival kit' and anything else that needed carrying as he was the skinniest and always lost any arm wrestling bouts.

'Where's the fizzless orange?' Barry said, groping around in an almost empty bag. 'Finished it off ages ago' Steve replied in a voice that was worried because he knew he would almost certainly be blamed.

'Why didn't you tell us?' Barry said, affirming Steve's fears.

'Bloody hell' said Barry, ' I'm so thirsty I could..'

'So am I, are you sure there's no orange left?' It was Les and all of a sudden all five of us were facing an agonising dying of thirst death.

And then I saw the empty, void of curtains house, with the big For Sale sign nailed to a wooden post beside the front door, a door that was slightly ajar.

'Come on I said and motioned the others to follow me.

'Where are we going ?' asked Les.

'Into that empty house' I replied and before Les could ask another stupid question I said, 'Houses have kitchens don't they and kitchens have sinks don't they and sinks have taps don't they?'

We all did bad impressions of the cast in 'Ice cold in Alex' rubbing our sweaty foreheads in the crooks of our arms and licking our lips whilst we made our way to the open door dreaming of drowning in tepid tap water.

The hat and coat hanging in the hallway should have given us a warning but the hollow echoes of the house's emptiness was enough to assure us that the house was indeed unoccupied.

Once in the kitchen we availed ourselves of tap water placing our mouths over the said taps and each getting several gobfulls.

When the sound of the man shouting obscenities at us from somewhere upstairs came terrifyingly to our ears it was each Cec for himself as we bundled to the front door and out into the road running for all we were worth..

If Steve had been a bit faster and not the lightest of us all he would not have been shoved aside and into the leafless spiky hedge running along the garden's edge, so obviously it was his own fault.

We were quite a distance down the lane before the lack of any sound from behind told us that we were not being chased.

Poor old Steve was probably being hung up in a tree somewhere according to an ancient Mortimer Common ritual, 'Death to thee who trespass into another's semi) but that again was his own fault, we had miles in the heat to walk back to occupy our minds.

Hours later we finally made it home and after drinking far too much water we all sat on the curb outside Les's house eating crabapples from a previous scrumping expedition.

'What are we gonna tell Steve's mum?'

It was Barry, selecting his third crabapple from the old duffle bag we always used on scrumping expeditions.

I had not really given the question much thought due to the fact that it was Steve's fault he got caught in the first place. I was still trying to convince myself of this when Steve casually walked up to us, bent over the duffle bag, picked out a crabapple, sat on the curb beside me and sunk his teeth deep into the fruits flesh.

All chewing ceased immediately as four sets of bewildered eyes rested on Steve's apple filled smug face.

'I told the bloke exactly what happened and he said poor kid and your mates left you to take all the blame, come on I'll give you a lift home in my car…and it was a B.M.W'

Barry snatched Steve's half eaten crabapple from out of his hand and without uttering a word threw it as far as he could down Gainsborough Road.

*

While we're on the subject of tortoises (let me relate a very sad story about one)

Tortoises were inexpensive in those days and most of the Cec's on the estate had one. I wanted one for my birthday so mum bought me one. I had three at different times although the first one I was given as far as I was concerned wasn't a tortoise at all but a turtle!! (I promise I will explain that particular conundrum later).

Stubby and Blodwin didn't know each other (one died before the other) but lived in the same cage, hutch, box, whatever you call the thing you keep a tortoise in. Blodwin died after a long (obviously too long hibernation) in the coal shed. Stubby lasted at least two terms of hibernation in the coal shed and the first tortoise that wasn't a turtle didn't last long enough to get a name. I thought the first tortoise my mum bought me was a turtle. It wasn't. It was actually a tortoise but I didn't know that because I'd never had a turtle or a tortoise. And tortoises don't last very long when you think they are turtles and you put them in a bucket of water. Sorry tortoises everywhere but it's your fault for looking like turtles.

*

Joe 90

We called them the Playing Fields which was odd considering it was only one field and all in all quite a small area containing swings, a slide, a seesaw, a witches hat all at the bottom of a sloping grassed area.
Completely cordoned off from Bute Street by a low wire fence and entrance gate, the customary way of entrance to said playing fields was to go straight along Gainsborough Road (where I and my hoard lived) and turn first right into Bute Street.
Going through the unadopted gravel lanes of the back garages was much more fun because of its 'No right of way' status, the potential of finding discarded bike parts and all sorts of other hidden treasures too inviting to us Cecs.

It didn't matter that going that way meant having to scale a ten foot fence, leaping from its top and tumbling down the grassy gradient to finally get to the playing fields, that just added to the fun of it all.

Like red Indians screaming and whooping we rode our mustangs down the slope towards the see saw and witches hat, dodging the huge rocks and towering cacti.

Mothers looked up at us from behind the relative safety of their pushchairs, pulling blankets up and over their tiny offspring and fathers closed their papers, put their cigarettes out on the ground and ran out to pluck their little kids from the prospects of being scalped by the marauding savages that had just appeared from nowhere.

Having reached the level ground of the play area in a cloud of swirling dust we tied our steeds to the metal frame of the swings and jostled for first go on the slide.

A slide that was never much of a slide to us Cecs, not high enough, not fast enough but we did have a remedy for one of those enoughs, a simple household candle, every council house had them in abundance.

After a vigorous, elbow grease consuming covering of candle wax and a few test pilot slidings to buff it up the said slide became a winter olympic ski jump.

With little friction on the bums of our already shiny short cotton trousers a great speed could be achieved for descent especially if the 'skier' did a skiers 'high hopping' leap' at the top of the slides steps and hurled himself into the air and braced himself for impact.

After a few more 'slide's at supersonic speeds it was fun standing back and watching the little ones flying down the highly polished slide surface and being ejected at high speed their tiny legs trying to keep up with the rest of their bodies as they flew through the air screaming 'mummy' at the tops of their voices.

*

His name was Pele and we all loved him, he was a bright yellow budgerigar (not a canary) and in the evenings Pele would be let out of his cage (with all of the room's windows closed) to fly freely around and land on our heads.

Dad was at work, my sisters were playing hopscotch out the front on the pavement and my brother was out helping the milkman on his rounds. The house was quiet until…

I could hear mum screaming from the back garden where I was digging up worms to go fishing. I ran into the front room to be greeted with the sight of mum standing rigid by Pele's open cage, holding the vacuum cleaner nozzle in one hand and the other tightly clamped to her mouth , stifling what without a doubt was further hysterical screams.

As I approached she took the hand from her mouth and made pointing gestures with her index finger between the open door of Pele's cage and the tiny black mouth of the vacuum cleaner hose.

I looked at one to the other and then I noticed the small yellow feathers drifting on the air from the breeze coming in from the back door and bigger feathers stuck to wires of the cage's open door.

I went rigid on the spot as it slowly dawned me what mum had just done.

A vision of Pele frantically flapping his wings with all his might against the immense suction power of the Electrolux Z345 was imprinted in my brain along with my mum's (it wasn't my fault) look in her terrified eyes.

I lowered myself to my knees snatching at the dual catches on each side of the vacuum cleaner that was now almost certainly the unwitting instrument of poor old Pele's gruesome demise.

With the back cover of the machine removed I held my breath realising that my eyes had been shut tight against the horrible sight that was about to greet me and then due to overwhelming morbid curiosity I opened them.

Pele was beakfirst flat against the Electrolux Z345's dust filter doing a brilliant impersonation of a spread eagle as if viewed from the back.

My mum was shouting in my ear 'Is he alive, is he alive ? Oh my God I've killed him, I was only doing what I always do, hovering all the muck of the bottom of his cage and then 'Phloop' Pele was gone'
I prised Pele off the filter and he immediately flew from my hand to his favourite perching place on top of the curtain pelmets.
Pele had survived the hoovering and lived for quite a time after and the featherless bald patch on the top of his head looked quite fetching after a while. Mum never used the Electrolux Z345 to clean his cage again.

*

My big brother Bob got a part time job helping out in the local butchers.
'Bob you'll be a butcher's boy and that's the way you'll stay, Bob you'll be a butcher's boy until your dying day' I would sing it at him all the time until he looked like he would hit me, obviously he was not a fan of Cliff Richard.
'Can you get me a pig's skull?' I pleaded with him time and time again. The thought of having a real skull on top of the little cabinet by my bed was awesome, I could learn all the names of the bones in it and impress my friends, it would be like having my own dinosaur fossil.

One day Bob came home looking all pleased with himself and handed me a grease stained bag. I dropped the severed hairy pig's ear on the floor and was nearly sick.
'It was the nearest I could find' said Bob.

*

Pogles Wood

'Peacock Farm' that's what we called it in those days, nowadays it's called the Beale Wildlife Park'. We called it Peacock Farm because it
had a lot of peacocks, calling out in their haunting cries and roaming free.
It had a lot of other birds in cages all over the place but the peacocks were our main interest, well to be precise peacock feathers were our main interest, well to be even preciser peacock tail feathers were our main interest.
We all craved a big tail feather as a keepsake, a souvenir, a trophy, a *'look what I've got and you haven't'* A peacock feather with an ocellus on it said Barry. What's an ocellus? said Les, 'I don't know' said Barry, but I want one. I told Barry I thought it was the thing that looked like an eye (the evil eye mum called it and added don't you dare bring one of those things in my house).
We found lots of feathers but never a peacock's tail feather and Barry's suggestion of running after them

and then stamping on their tails didn't seem quite right, besides they could run a lot faster and were far more zig-zagier than us.

*

We started off for Peacock Farm on a lovely sunny morning, Bob, Les, Malcolm, me and Barry, peddling away on our virtually hand made bikes (belated apologies to all those silly pupils who left their bikes in the bikesheds of a certain school over the summer holidays).

It was quite a distance to Theale from our estate so our saddlebags were full of essential items i.e. crisps, pork pies, bottles of corona, mars bars and of course our catapults.

The thought of taking a puncture outfit was not even considered which was a pity really because halfway there Bob got a front wheel puncture, well to be honest a gaping hole in his tyre would be a better description

(those silly pupils who left their bikes in the bikesheds of a certain school over the summer holidays should have taken far more care of them !)

P.s. We never purloined whole bikes, just certain bits we needed for ours.

Anyway, there we were in the middle of nowhere and Bob was potentially bikeless unless we could come up with a remedy and the surrounding fields of hay supplied us with that remedy.

Using Les's swiss army knife we opened the blade for getting stones out of horses hooves (it really didn't matter to Les if we broke that one off Les said because he didn't have a horse) and used it to lever the front tyre halfway off its rim. Then having tugged out the useless innertube and disposing of it, we pulled up handfuls of hay from the fields and stuffed it with our fingers into the entire gap between tire and wheel rim. Folding the tyre back onto its rim over the hay was easy and Bob's bike was now fit enough for the 'Tour de France'.

*

February 1943 four bombs hit Reading Town centre courtesy of the German Luftwaffe, not that I was around at the time to see it of course but we Cecs believed that one of the bombs provided us with a big dark hole to explore.

The Devil's Pit was the name we gave to this big dark hole and although occupied by all sorts of ghosts, spirits and devils (it stood to reason because obviously thousands of people were blown to bits in it) it was irresistible to us already dirty kneed Cec's. Below ground level and surrounded by dense bushes and tall trees it was always a dark, dank and gloomy place, carpeted by mud that never dried and puddles that only deepened. It had an inhospitable aura that drew us Cecs like snakes to a snakepit but always together, never alone. A place to practise with our catapults, air pistols, bows and arrows (but we soon got fed up losing our arrows to the trees) and thick impenetrably thick bushes.

The Devils Pit was situated opposite Prospect Park with the A4 (Bath Road) running between them. Connecting the Park to the pit and running under the road was a tunnel, a brick built tunnel we called 'The Tunnel of Death' (what else?) and it was this tunnel that supplied a lot of our amusement.

The park end of the tunnel was partially blocked with overgrown bramble bushes and nettles; we took it in turns to run stooped low through this black, rat infested hole, the only source of light being the one at the end of it!! I never saw a single rat but what would be the point of running through a black rat infested tunnel if there were no rats infesting it?

The pit side was far more enticing with a bobsleigh shaped concrete slope leading from the road level down to the pit's floor just the job for any wheeled easily obtained vehicle, a shopping trolley fitting the bill more than adequately.

It wouldn't take too many cuts, abrasions and bruises due to spills before we abandoned the shopping trolley and put it out of sight into the nettles.

The Devil's Pit was beginning to lose its allure, not just because we were fed up with always going home soaking wet and covered in mud but somehow we felt our mums weren't too happy about that fact either. Besides that it was Chestnut season and Tutts Clump, Trash Green and Uften Nervet were beckoning us, the Chestnut centres of the entire world and Reading.

*

Aquaman

Time for the bikes and the maintenance they required i.e. spraying WD40 on every surface you could reach and some you couldn't.
We were ready to set off for the above locations armed with anything heavy and suitable for throwing into the branches of the Chestnut trees.
Unlike conkers (of which there is mention of later in my scribbles). Chestnuts are edible and as far as we were concerned a luxury, they were free, plentiful and cookable even to us uncookerers.
Loaded up with bags of freshly scrumpied Chestnuts we rode home preparing in our minds the bonfire we would make for the roasting of our nuts.
It is highly recommended that each chestnut is pierced with a fork several times before putting them on the fire, but it's much more fun if you don't, they shoot everywhere!

Roasted chestnuts are delicious and a good remedy for diarrhoea if you eat enough of them (useful if you are loose after eating too many scrumpied crabapples).

*

Monday was washing day, mum would always do the washing on Monday. The clothes were boiled and washed by hand in the Copper (more about that particular vessel later) and then put through the mangle to squeeze them dry. The mangle fascinated me for two reasons.
 1). Because of the mess it made of insects when you put them through it.
2). Because when I later slammed mum's thumb in the train door on the platform at Paddington Station the Doctor told me her thumb looked like it had been put through the mangle.
Paddington Station…'Kim, open the door'
'Why?'
'My thumb's in it'
I'll never forget my mum's composure as we left for A&E St.Mary's Hospital, Paddington, her hand wrapped up in a clean British Rail tea towel.

P.S. A hanging offence on the Southcote Estate and dare I say any other Estate in this fine land of ours.

Lighting your fire when someone has their washing on the line...it was never done.

*

It was a beautiful dog, a sort of labradory looking dog, sandy coloured with big brown eyes, a forever wagging tail and no collar. It followed me and Bob all the way from the sweetshop in Coronation Square then into the playing fields where we both saw for the first time in our lives the sign that had always been there (we had many a time chained our bikes to it) No Dogs Allowed.

It wasn't our dog so it didn't count so we let it in. It barked at us when we swang on the swing, jumped up at us when we slid on the slide and ate half of our cheese and onion crisps when we sat on the grass. We told it to go home but it didn't want to.

'What are we going to do with it?' It was Bob, and the dog heard him and jumped up and pushed him over onto his back. We ran around the small park and the dog chased us barking and going down on its front legs when we stopped to pat its head.

The dog made us laugh but it was getting dark, nearly time for tea.

We couldn't take it home mum was scared of dogs (I have never been too comfortable with them either) and she would never let it in the house.

'I've got an idea' Bob said, which was weird because as far as I was concerned my brother Bob never had any ideas.

He dished deep into his pocket and retrieved his last 3 tuppences and we headed off to the phone box on Southcote Lane, the dog bouncing off our bare legs as we ran.

We found the number in the huge phone book's yellow pages and rang the RSPCA. I let the dog into the kiosk so we could hear over its constant barking and whining from outside.

I watched him dial, hesitate, then push button A. It was a good thing he was always phoning his girlfriend, he knew just what to do.

'Hello, we've got a dog and it's not ours'

I could only hear my brother on the phone but it was obvious he'd got through to the RSPCA because he was talking all posh.

'We found it, well it found us really'

'Outside the sweetshop in Coronation Square'

'Reading'

'We waited for ages but nobody…'

'No we..'

'No, no collar or nothing..'

'No, its not hurt, it can run and everything'

'Like a labrador but smaller and skinnier'

'It ate a lot of our cheese and onion crisps'

'Ok we won't but..'

'No we can't, mums scared of dogs and any…'

``We don't don't know, we just..'
'Why not, we..?'
'Oh, flipping 'ell'
Bob put another tuppence in the slot but dropped his last one on the floor. I tried to pick it up but there was too much writhing dog in the way, he was still talking..
'We can't, we have to..'
'No we don't know anybody I told..'
'But can't you send..?'
Bob was shaking his head from side to side and swearing as he put the phone down and looked at us both looking at him.
He had run out of tuppences and it was getting darker outside.
'I think they will close soon anyway,' he said, patting the dog on the head as if he was talking to it, not me.
We left the phone kiosk, or were pulled out of it by the dog I can't remember which and walked away.
After a while Bob went back to get his tuppence mumbling about the loss of four halfpenny chews and when he got back it was darker.
An idea had occurred to me and the relief was so that we ran all the way to the Calcot Road, the dog tugging me forward as if it knew where we were heading for. It didn't take us long to find a house that looked promising and the lamppost nearby lit up the front of it which was handy. The curtains were drawn and lit up from a light inside, its occupants were in and probably watching Emergency Ward Ten.

Just the job. A six foot hedge ran along all three sides of the front garden with a tall gate the only entrance or exit. Bob volunteered me for the task saying I was smaller and harder to see in the dark therefore it was obvious it had to be me.

For the first few steps the dog needed tugging as it stood looking back wondering why Bob was walking away slowly in the opposite direction.

I shouted in a whisper 'come on boy' in a happy sounding voice and the dog followed me through the gate and into the garden.

The idea was to ring the doorbell, leave the dog and get out through the gate as fast as I could, leaving the people watching Emergency Ward Ten an unexpected doggie present. It didn't happen entirely like that because I didn't get to ring the doorbell, I ran out of nerve and just as quickly I ran out of the garden, slammed the gate behind me and caught up with my brother.

'How did it go?' he said breathlessly as by now we were both running.

'Fine' I lied Fine'

*

Five o'clock Club

It would become the Dee Road Estate, a huge sprawling estate that contained hundreds of houses that were exact replicas of each other and thousands of people who were also replicas of each other. But for now it was just a building site, a building site that looked like a bomb site, a site for sore eyes. Half finished houses, half finished roads and half finished builders. I had been given one of the most important jobs on the entire site. Dad had given me a pot of brown goo and a brush and precise directions. I was to visit each skeleton of a house and with my pot of brown goo and my brush paint over every gnarl and notch on the bare wood surfaces of every door and window pane.

It was a job with heavy responsibility but he knew I was up to it, he had previously counted all the gnarls and notches and there were six million of them, it would take me days.

One identical empty house after the other all dry dusty and smelling of painty things.

I was down to about 5,999,725 gnarls and notches still to do, I could hardly hear Tony Blackburn on the tinny radio or the constant swearing of the workers as they banged nails into everything they could see in the half built house I'd left 'done' about half an hour ago and I was bored silly. Brushing brown goo over gnarls and notches requires little skill and soon becomes no fun at all. Well it probably was a lot more fun than standing on a huge shiny nail sticking up from some planks of wood on the floor.

I could not move, something in the bottom of my leg seized up and I could not pull my foot up. It didn't hurt at first and then it did, alot.

I remember thinking that I was going to get into a lot of trouble for getting blood all over the nice clean planks of wood and the floorboards below.

I shouted as loud as I could but Tony Blacburn was making far more noise than me and the workers were still happy banging in nails.

'What's going on here then nipper?'

He was huge standing in the doorway silhouette against the light of the door that wasn't there. Even through my eyes that were blurred by tears I could see he was a cowboy. His gun was strapped to his side and he had a knife in his belt and I could imagine his horse called Silver tied up on the railings just outside the doorless doorway. 'Now what have you been getting up to nipper?'

He was walking toward me talking softly and talking a lot and I began to wonder why a cowboy would be wearing a bright yellow hat.

When he bent down and slipped both his hands under my armpits he was still talking softly, when he jerked me up quickly his gun fell from his belt and turned into a hammer. My foot was on fire and the pain made me dizzy but I still looked back as he carried me out of the house for Silver but he wasn't anywhere to be seen.

They took me to the hospital where I had a tetanus jab and got patched up. I never did get know who the cowboy was but 'Mighty grateful partner here's a'hoping we meet up on the prairie again someday'

*

The pools man, the milkman, the butchers man, the baker, the man who sold pink paraffin from a big pink paraffin lorry, the coal man, the postman, the man who offered to sharpen our knives and garden shears, Gordon who drove a converted-into-a-grocer-shop-coach man, the Corona van man, the rag and bone man, Mormons, Jehovah's Witnesses, salesmen of all descriptions and many more called at our house on a regular basis but of the lot only two come to mind. The insurance man being one…he reminded me of Hyram Holliday, a television star of the time (please google him). Although his job was collecting the insurance money from mum he always asked for me and I was happy to talk to him because he was an angler, or in my parlance a fisherman. He would tell me stories of the huge fish he'd caught, how he caught them, what bait he used, what breaking strain line he caught them on, how long it took him to land them, (I think I must have been writing in my head 'The Broadwater Trilogy' my series of books that I would eventually write years later) as he spoke.

'I tell you what' he said, 'You should join YOTAC'
'Join YOTAC' I said, looking up at him in awe.
'Yes, YOTAC ' he said 'For you it will only be a
shilling a month'
'Only a shilling a month?' I said.
'Yes' he said ' And you get one of these little
membership books' he said, waving a little green
book with gold lettering on it that seemed to appear
from nowhere in front of my face.
'Cor' I said 'Yes I said 'I'll join YOTAC'
'Great' he said,'I'll bring the application form next time
I come'
'Ok' I said to his back as he walked away.
A little green book with gold lettering on the front and
I'll be a member I thought.
And then another thought struck me and I shouted
across the garden at him as he walked away...'What
does YOTAC mean?'
'Ye Olde Thames Angling Club' he shouted back.
'Cor' I said.

*

Noggin the Nog

It took two buses to get there and a day off school,
those were just two of the things I liked about it. I had
a lazy left eye, a squint. When I looked at you with
one eye I was looking for the bus with the other. It

was quite pronounced and the doctors thought they could do something to rectify it, strengthen the muscles in it and exercise it. So every few weeks mum took me to the Royal Berkshire Hospital in Reading and it took two buses and a day off school to get there.

The apparatus looked like a periscope to me but it had two eyepieces and wasn't a periscope.

'Put your chin on here Kim, look into the eyepieces and tell me what you can see'

'A picture of a house'

'Does it have windows and a door?'

'No'

Something clicked and the lady in a white coat said..

'Right, Now can you see the windows and a door?'

'Yes but they are not on the house'

'Right Kim, hold this lever in your hand and move it until the windows and the door are on the house'

'Ok'

'Are the windows and the door on the house now Kim?'

'Yes, no, yes, no, yes, no, it just depends if I want them to be or not'

And besides I think I've fallen in love with you.

I didn't say that last bit but I wanted to.

A few more 'exercises' and talking about this and that and we were back on the bus home stopping at the market to buy my treat for being a good boy…half a pint of shrimps measured in a half pint beer glass

which I loved to eat the proper way by pulling them apart with my fingers and eating raw.
Good for your eyes apparently.
I've since had an operation on my squint and now unless I am very tired I don't see a bus coming when I speak to anyone any more and I'm going to marry that nurse when I get older.

*

Rock cake made in a huge baking tray, we'd fight over the hard sugary end bits, St.Helenian Bread and Dance sandwiches, tomato, egg, bacon, chilli paste (a unique taste from mums island home), sandwiches of all kinds,(bar marmite, no one liked marmite) jam, marmalade, banana, sugar, salad cream, peanut butter, corned beef, plain crisps with an Oxo cube sprinkled over, rhubarb crumble made from the massive trifid looking rhubarb plant in our back garden, dumplings covered in golden syrup (from a green tin with a lion on it swatting flies) just a few gastric memories of my childhood..oh yeah and when mum was in hospital dad made us liver, just liver, two enormous slabs of liver, nothing else !!

*

Captain Scarlet and the Mysterons

He said his name was Searle, but dad and mum called him John. He worked at the same place as dad but he lived in a place called Mortimer which was a long way away. He would ride his bike to our house, leave it in our shed and then get the same bus to work as dad did. After work he would pick up his bike to ride it back to Mortimer.

Mum and dad gave him permission to do this because he often brought them bags of vegetables, he never came into the house though, he never needed to.

Searle was an astronaut but he couldn't tell people because he had to keep it a secret, he was building a rocket in his own shed in Mortimer and said (he didn't want people disturbing him because his rocket was nearly finished). Sometimes when he was too early for the bus he would show me photos of his nearly finished rocket and charts of where he was going to travel to in the universe.

When he suddenly stopped leaving his bike in our shed I realised he must have taken off...I looked for a while on the news but then remembered he'd told me it was all secret..I was going to ask dad but in time I forgot.

Looking back I'm convinced Searle was telling me the truth, his truth at any rate.

*

There were thousands of them, I'd never seen so many people in one place, men and ladies, old and young. Where the cars should have been and always were there were people. Some held flags with black and white patterns on them, an upside down catapult with a line running down the middle of it. Others had banners but they were all walking towards Calcot..It was dark, it was cold but there were so many people and they just kept coming. Mum told me it was a Ban the bomb march from London to Aldermaston 1958.
I got to stay up quite late that night.

*

Saturday morning and the news spread like wildfire on the Southcote Council Estate. We didn't know her name (and to be honest didn't care) but she lived down Brunel Road and for a thruppenny bit you could buy one of her delicious homemade toffee apples. Bikes peddled by knees scraped and snotty nosed boys and girls from all over the estate appeared as if by magic in a hurry to have first pick.
First pick I hear you say, surely a toffee apple is much like any other toffee apple. Wrong, some apples in the process of being toffee coated had been over endowed with said toffee thus allowing it congeal at the bottom forming a large 'skirt' of chewy, teeth clogging, golden and to us eternally ravenous kids a meal in itself.

I can still feel the exciting sensations of biting through the brittle glasslike outer shell, my mouth filling with the soft flesh of the apple secreted inside. Sitting over the saddle of my bike with apple juice and toffee goo dribbling down my chin, casually swatting at the growing number of wasps flying around my head, I was in heaven.

*

Vision On

We needed a big stone, can or empty bottle to put on the kerb to act as the stumps, one that would stand out for all of us Cecs to see when we ran to score a run.

I climbed over the fence into the building site and after a few minutes found our marker, an empty Orangeade Corona half bottle, I climbed back and raised it in the air for Yvonne to see. As I neared her she raised her hands so I threw it over towards her so she could catch it and she didn't.

It hit her in the face. All the others stared at me and then at her and the thought struck us all at the same time. No French cricket for us tonight, not with all that blood on Yvonne's forehead. I saw his bike first, then his uniform, finally his helmet, to my abject fear the policeman was dismounting and making his way to Yvonne who was making silly crying noises and holding her head, the Orangeaid half Corona bottle sitting against the kerb, where unbroken it had rolled over to.

Then I noticed all at once that the would-be cricket team, the policeman and Yvonne, were all pointing at me and gesturing at me. I quickly looked away and was soon running towards my house, at speed.

I made it to the back door and was inside before the policeman arrived as I feared he was going to.

Mum had come out of the kitchen just in time to see me disappear between the front room wall and the sofa, the gap being only just adequate for a small and skinny boy my size.

I heard mum and the policeman whispering and then the policeman's blood curdling voice boomed out.

'Where is he?'

The policeman sounded angry and I could imagine he had his truncheon in one hand and his big shiny gun in the other.

'It's no good hiding from me I'll find him'

'What are you going to do if you find him?'

It was my mum's voice and she didn't sound exactly on my side.

'Might have to take him to prison'

'She's ok, looks a lot worse than it is' (Yvonne's mum)

It was a female voice I didn't recognise but it sounded just great.

'Ok" I heard the policeman say.

'But he'd better not do anything like that again, he'd better behave himself in future'
I'm sure I saw a fleeting smile on the policeman's lips as he dragged me out from behind the sofa by my bumper boots.

*

Sunday morning and the battle of the Southcote Estate Cecs would be won on the playing fields of Prospect Park, or so we all hoped.
From as early as 07.30 the game would commence, Cecs would arrive from all corners of the Southcote Estate and other Cecs from as far afield as Tilehurst, Calcot and Coley.
Dressed in whatever apparel would pass as a football kit and shoes or boots that had long since worn out on the hard concrete of school playgrounds the game would commence (if someone had managed to procure a half decent football).
The hub of the players would be the locals, by locals I mean the Cecs in Southcote who were close enough to the park to have had their Cornflakes, Shredded Wheat or toast and jam early enough in the morning.
The 'pitch' would be marked out by means of piles of jumpers for goalposts (growing bigger as more and more Cecs arrived) and more jumpers marking out each of the four corners.

Sometimes us Cecs would venture further into the park where the proper league football pitches were already marked out with white lines and if
we were particularly lucky the goalposts were still standing.
(they were usually taken down after 'proper' league games had been played.
One big disadvatage however about playing on these league pitches was that our football games could easily last for 3-4 hours and said pitches were in the middle of the park in open space making them quite a distance from the nearest loos or of course any convenient trees (another pun intended) Our usual means of relieving ourselves (when playing on our jumper marked out pitch) was a quick dash to Bluebell woods which was only a few yards away. Bluebell woods was not a real wood but a cluster of trees with a muddy path running betwixt them and was also well known for not having Bluebells in it. Having marked out the pitch and picked the teams which was done in the fairest way possible, the two bigger stronger Cecs taking turns to choose who he wanted on his team until all that was left were the skinny kids or those with two left feet, wearing glasses, teeth braces and shivering in the cold. (poor old 'Spanner Legs, Spanners for short, always being in that particular group) the game would commence.
An hour into it, eight new Cecs, have joined in, one has been summoned home by his mum shouting at

him from the park's fence that he's got to take his sister to Sunday School like she told him this morning, a fight nearly broke out because of dirty sliding leg biting tackle and the score is 41 to 27 we think.

By now the goal hangers* had been identified and threatened with death, a small spectator group had formed (mainly girls and old men reliving their youth shouting 'Well played old chap' and 'He was clearly offside ref'. Strange because we didn't have a referee or bother with offside)   * Goal hangers were as their name probably suggests, players that were either too lazy, too fat or too inept to 'run the pitch in normal play' but stay in a forward position hoping to receive the ball and with it head towards the goal unimpeded.

An hour and a half into the game, more Cecs have joined in and some have left but no-one is counting or noticing and the goalposts are now three feet high and growing. A rare pause is called while a player is down and injured, rolling around on the grass like a proper footballer and ignored by everyone.

It's now something like 57 to 36. Some little know it all, irritating budding mathematician once suggested that we simply simplify the scoring by subtracting one score from the other hence making it now 11 to nil. That was ok until someone on the losing side scored a goal, should it be 11 to 1 or 10 to nil..should the 10 keep going down or the nil go up? This was even more confusing and easier to cheat with as far as us Cecs were concerned and then a shout went up 'Goal' great 57 to 36.

2 hours into the game and the number of players on each side is becoming less and less as the desire amongst either side to win is diminished by the growing realisation that no-one cares and besides no-one really remembers what the score is.

Outside interest start to creep in like 'Oh look, that's Carol and Jane watching from under that tree' or 'the weather is getting better for fishing' or probably, most likely 'I'm starving!'

More and more Cecs start to disappear, the balance of difference between team abilities becomes wider and unequal and more disturbing than any of this, the goal and corner post begin to disappear.

The epic game of football for that Sunday morning is finally over.

Years later I revisited that part of Prospect Park and stood for a while to listen to the excited shouts of the players, to watch my old Cec friends chasing after the ball and as one putting their arms in the air and screaming 'goal' at the top of their voices' I stood for a long while, but I never got picked to play, there was no-one doing the picking, there was no-one waiting to be picked.

*

Tales of the river bank

Kevin and Michael were up at their bedroom window, my brother (Bob) and I up at ours. We had spent most of the afternoon laying the string across both our back gardens over the tall wire fence around the fish pond and between the trees.

Using my mum's clothes prop we took it in turns to pass the string ends up to each other at the windows and once it was in our grip pulled it into our respective bedrooms. Now with the string between us we pulled it tight until it was high enough to be horizontal with the gardens below and at the same height as us.

We banged six inch nails into the bottoms of the tin cans we had rescued and cleaned from the rubbish bins earlier then pulled them out leaving small jagged holes. We threaded the string through the holes and tied the ends in a tight knot big enough to stop it being pulled through.

The cans thus connected, we waited for darkness to fall because sound travelled better at night and besides if we wanted to talk to each other during the daylight it was a simple matter of walking to each other's houses and knocking on the door, besides that was nowhere near as much fun.

At last darkness fell and as planned Kevin and Michael flashed their bedroom light three times to announce that they were ready.

Bob picked up our can and waited for Michael to do the same at his end and together they gently pulled it to take up all the slack.

Bob put the can to his mouth, Michael put his can to his ear and I gripped the curtain in anticipation.

Hi Michael it's me Bob, are you receiving me, over?'

'Yes' said Micheal, Loud and clear, over'

Bob and I grinned at each other in the dull light, 'Yes he said 'Bloody hell it works, it actually works'

Then he lowered the can, gave me a quizzical look and said..

'What do I say now ?'

Which is probably what Alexander Graham Bell said when he patented the first telephone.

*

It was a good three quarters of an hour from my front door, a fair walk carrying a plastic bag full of swimming paraphernalia, cheese or peanut butter sandwiches, bottles of coke, crisps and dragging along your sisters. (It was after all a whole day out) You went along the Bath Road down Berkeley Avenue and down a grassy lane and where you least expected to see a swimming pool there was a swimming pool.

Coley Park Swimming Baths, we used to joke..4d to get in and a shilling to get out. Being completely open air it was always freezing cold.

It was here where I learnt to swim (underwater before on the surface) and where I nearly drowned (more of both later).

Coley Park Swimming Baths (built 1880, closed 1974, and originally mens bathing only) was a huge concrete structure with wide paved areas either side of the main pool and what can only be described as a long series of sheds for changing in.

A wooden bench ran along the inside of these sheds for dropping your clothes on, above your head was the sky which was usually grey, overcast and full of smoke from the nearby steel factory.

For modesty reasons a green tarpaulin dangled from hooks on a metal 'A' frame that could be pulled across to save the girls' blushes and the boys' curiosities.

The pool was the regulation rectangular shape but in the middle of the deep end was a protruding 'V' of concrete whereupon sat the wide diving board. I found that if I took a running leap from the side of the pool and did a shallow dive, I could reach the edge of this 'V' underwater and by placing my hands, palms flat against its rough uneven sides I could paddle myself up to the surface.

I started at a narrower angle until I gained confidence enough to surface just a few feet from the wall and doggy paddle the rest. Using this tactic I finally learnt to swim where most people swim, on the pool's surface.

On schooldays us Cecs were treated to a bit of luxury of sorts, we were taken to Coley Park Swimming Baths by bus, it made no difference to the water's temperature but you didn't have to shiver all the way back home or pay an entrance fee.

As we were led into the pool area each and everyone of us had to queue to put our naked feet into a big aluminium bucket full of a type of disinfectant, once that was done we were led to the water's edge and invited to *get in as soon as possible as we haven't got all day*

Her name was Rosemary and she coincidently lived on the same road as me in Southcote, Gainsborough Road. I never went 'out' with her but like most girls I met I would like to have done, if given the remotest chance.

The proper swimmers in our school were at the deep end showing off, us learners in the shallow end wearing or using all sorts of buoyancy aids, mine being an inflatable ring.

Am I the only person in the world to have done this? I'm certain I can't possibly be.

With graceful ease I turned my swimming aid into a drowning aid. With the ring in position under my armpits I made forward breastroke motions in the water with my arms.

Everything was going swimmingly (excuse the blatant pun) until I pushed myself from the bottom of the pool with my feet in an attempt to do what I was attempting to do and swim. As I did this the water had other ideas, as I endeavoured to swim it tried to pull me back to the pool floor causing the ring to slip down a few inches over my boney ribs towards my trunks. Not heeding what was an obvious warning I pushed forward again. As I was making progress in the water, the buoyancy ring did what it was designed to do, namely keep me buoyant, but due to my struggling the ring was keeping the wrong part of me buoyant

Eventually the buoyancy ring made its way to my shins where it became far less a potential lifesaver more a potential life taker.

I was horizontal on the surface, my lower body beautifully buoyed by the ring around my ankles, my upper body going into panic mode for any kind of buoyancy at all and my mouth was filled with chlorine flavoured water.

And then all of a sudden someone's shoulders appeared in front of my squinting eyes and miraculously those shoulders were within easy reaching distance. I grabbed hold of them as if my life depended on it, which of course it did and by pulling myself towards the owner of those shoulders and forcing my legs down towards the pool's floor I managed to persuade the ring to travel back to their rightful place, up and under my armpits. I often wonder if the owner of those life saving shoulders, a girl called Rosemary, has any idea of the role her shoulders played in my life because I'm afraid my macho pride would never let me tell her.

*

Looking out of the front room window we saw Jackie, Barry, Malcolm, Carol, Leslie and Yvonne in the gloom of twilight on the road outside our house....and with nothing on the telly the urge to join them was overwhelming.
Sandra was first out of the door, followed by Serena then Jackie, still eating a slab of a 'bread and dance sandwich' (to be revealed later in my book unless you've already thrown the book away of course)..and I followed Jackie as nonchalantly as possible because no way did I want to play any childish games, I've got far better things to do.
The night was darkening, the lamp post arching halfway over the road lit up a couple of the road squares and left the ones further away in the shade until the next identical lamp post took over and illuminated its own couple of squares.Thus the road was intermittently illuminated.
The squares in the road were segments of cement separated by thin black strips of pitch or tar (great for

digging up and sticking things together or weighting model aeroplanes) All these sections of squares were the same length and width bordered by kerb stones made especially to prop your bicycles up by its pedals. This was Gainsborough road but could have been a thousand other roads on the Southcote estate.

'Let's play 'Film Stars' suggested Leslie Brown and I agreed for two reasons 1. I fancied her 2. She lived right opposite us and her dad had once rescued me from a locked and jammed bedroom, but that will come later.

Rules of said 'Films Stars'...pay attention as failing to comply could result in tantrums and shouts of 'I'm not playing any more, you cheat, I'm going home, which was usually five or less houses away'

The one 'In' stands one side of the road on the kerb whilst the guessers stand opposite on the other kerb. The 'In' then whispers (quite loudly) the initials of a film or pop star.

R.O.

Much mincing to and fro or stepping up and down the kerb as the guessee tries to guess without the other guessees knowing or hearing what the opposing guessee might be guessing.

After a while with the tension mounting almost to hysterics it is ok for the guessees, if no other guessee has guessed correctly to request the 'In' to take two steps towards the guessees and onto the road and to reveal the name in a louder whisper..this is done several times until there is a sudden stampede amongst the guessees and they start throwing themselves across the road regardless as to whether a motor vehicle wants to use it at the same time.

The fun begins when two or more guessees have come up with the answer at the same time because the rule states that once a guessee has guessed they must traverse the road twice before giving the In their answer.

Roy Orbison I shout.

My turn to be 'In'.

This is all done of course under the light of said lamp post to give motorists a fair chance of braking before hitting and killing one of us kids.

*

Top Cat

The roads on the Southcote Estate lent themselves to all types of games for us Cecs being floodlit at night by lampposts and made with large squares of concrete laid with pitch poured between the gaps. The roads also had kerbs running along the sides about 8 inches high that acted as 'ball boundaries' So in effect we had numerous identical playing pitches already marked out for us to adapt our games to. Cricket, we used the base of the lamppost as wickets, rounders, the four corners of a square of concrete to run around having hit the ball and football tennis, (one of my favourites using a football as a tennis ball and your feet as a racquet) the pitch in the gaps acting as the net, albeit it a very low net but adequate as a guide to where the net should be. Apart from us being annoyed by the neighbours constantly opening their doors and shouting how much we annoyed them we had very little to annoy us apart from passing cars and motorbikes which annoyed us immensely.

*

We were Scott and Oakes on our first expedition. We would set up a base camp (my back garden) wait until the cover of darkness and then venture out with our sixpences in our pockets for vital supplies i.e. Strawberry Flavoured Milk in little waxed cartons from the vending machine on the Bath road.
According to my trusty Timex which we could see thanks to Les's 1s and 6d Woolworths plastic Ever Ready torch it was 03.30 hrs. As we climbed over the wire fence into the back fields and around the grounds of the old people's homes our eyes were alert for bears, werewolves, ghouls and blokes with bright hi vis jackets with Security written on them.

When we arrived at the Bath Road it looked so alien it being virtually car and peopleless, the occasional big lorry passed its driver giving us strange looks as he thundered away into the night.

But it was the silence that stirred us, well the silence and the eerie sight of houses in darkness with only one or two lights dotted about.

Neither of us really wanted Strawberry Flavoured Milk at that time of morning but it was what we had come for, it was our mission, so when we finally reached the milk vending machine and in turn deposited our sixpences in the small silver slot, it was almost a mission accomplished

We pushed the red illuminated button (Strawberry Milk) and stood back in excited anticipation.

First came the dull thud as the full carton fell from somewhere in the innards of the machine and then the loud CLUNK as our prize fell into the big aluminium tray at the vending machine's base.

As I bent to open the tray to take out my purchase I noticed the car on the opposite side of the road had stopped and blue and red lights were flashing on its roof.

The policeman approaching us from the car was at least twenty feet tall and swung a battle axe in his hands.

'Now what are you two little buggers doing out here at this hour ? He bellowed.

We told him about our mission to get Straw
Flavoured Milk, he looked at the vending machine,
the cartons in our handstand and then at us.
The battle axe disappeared somewhere in his black
apparel, he shrunk somewhat and said..
'Come on I'll give you a lift home'

We got a lift back to our respective houses that night
and one hell of a reception from our parents
I hope the policeman enjoyed the Strawberry
Flavoured milk we left on the back seat of his car.

*

'Mum said I could, you Serena, and Jackie did it last
night so it's my turn tonight, it is half my tent after all'
There was no arguing with Sandra, besides I wasn't
that bothered, I had another idea. I had spent the
afternoon putting the teepee up, three long bamboo
canes tied at the top forming a triangular shaped,
Indian style teepee, lacking in room but surely
enough for one, me. Bright yellow in colour with red
buffaloes printed on three sides it was a thirty bob
bargain from Woollies paid for with money from my
paper round.
'Mum we like sleeping out, talking girly talk and
giggling, why does he have to spoil it?'

'Let him put his tent up, don't worry, it's too small to sleep in, he's scared of the dark and he won't last long out there on his own'.

Huh, that's what she thinks I thought.

In our respective tents as the night drew in I could hear my siblings giggling between themselves talking and rustling in their sleeping bags. Soon it would be even darker and I could have my revenge, soon I could have my fun, soon I could scare the hell out of them.

Nearby I could hear them, rustling their sleeping bags and I could watch their torch lights dancing on the tents thin walls.

Soon it would be even darker and I could have my revenge. The shadows on my own tents' thin walls were just the bushes moved by the breeze and they didn't bother me, no not at all.

It must be time soon but they were still muttering to each other, all I had to do was just stay under the single blanket and wait, the distant sound was just someone's dog padding about in the backfields. On its own in the dark. It seemed like an age of waiting but I could still hear the girls chatting albeit in a whisper, they seemed too happy to be scared yet, so I would wait a bit longer and try to ignore the shivering.

My teepee was suddenly swamped in light, I jumped up from my sleeping bag, my head turning this way and that, chasing the shadows that were at once dancing all around the garden, my heart thudding in my chest. And as quickly as it came the light disappeared and a black like no other black filled my eyes.

Mum had turned the kitchen light on and off and returned to the front room, but the black stayed with me and the dog in the backfields started to whimper and then to wail and then to growl and its owner came out of the earth holding a whip in blood covered hands and it was getting colder much colder and the bushes had moved closer to my teepee which had started to tear down one side and my sisters weren't whispering any more they were sitting outside of their tent crouching around a huge steaming, cauldron wearing pointy hats and stirring something I couldn't see but was red with bones floating in it and I was banging on the back door, let me in mum let me in…!

*

Scooby Doo

She lived on a posh road (Worcester Close) and her name was Beverley. I fell in love with her the first time I saw her, something about her eyes and her brand new BMX. I'd ride my excuse for a bike slowly past her house and looking away but somehow

staring in her direction, I hoped she would be in her garden. And then one day she was. My sister had told me Beverley told her she liked me. That was enough, my heart beating too fast and my palms all sweaty. I slowed my bike (resisting the urge to do a flamboyant wheelie up to her garden wall (so it seemed I must have had a modicum of etiquette) I squeaked over to her…
'Hello Beverley, do you want to go out with me?"
'Ok' she answered, nonchalantly.
We never did get around to it (her going out with me, I mean) but she did say yes, and that was enough for me to tell all the rest of the Cecs..The beautiful Beverley from the posh Worcester Close had said to me yes.

*

The foundations were being built and the walls of it were two bricks wide and a few feet high, just high enough for us Cecs to climb up and balance on. Neil got up behind me and because I was taking my time going forward and he wanted to go faster he pushed me in the back...just as I decided to quicken my own pace.
His outstretched hands missed my back and he accomplished what he had wanted to do, which was to go forward faster. He did a sort of dance through

mid air and with nothing to stop him (because I had moved forward faster) he landed teeth first on the two bricks wide wall. He lost his two front upper teeth, made a hell of a mess of his lips and weeks later when he was able to speak again he blamed me. I think he still does.

They were building an old people's home on our 'backfields' and us Cecs were not at all happy about it. This land was ours, overgrown with nettles, brambles, bushes, small trees and the occasional supermarket trolley it was our domain. Backing onto the backs of our back gardens it was accessible by climbing any barrier your parents had built to prevent you gaining any access to it, it belonged to us. It was where we had our 'stone fights', a crazy game of cowboys and indians where guns and bows and arrows were replaced by stones that we threw at each other whilst hiding behind the many hillocks and small bushes.

The sight of a well aimed stone hitting a sandy outcrop and sending up a cloud of dust was music to my eyes.

Bang, bang, followed by the odd 'arrhhgg' sound filling the air was music to my ears and the theatrical hand over heart diving to the ground music to my imagination.

Sandra was an Indian, she wore a patch over one eye, an injury from a former battle, Barry a cowboy, who threw his knife and could hit an eagle's eye from

20 yards and I was a gunslinger who didn't really belong in a cowboy Indian / battle but no-one seemed to mind. The battles would rage until, 1) we ran out of stones to throw, which was never going to happen, 2) someone took a bullet (stone) for real and had to leave the prairie for a clean up with germolene and a sticking plaster 3) a Commanding officer from one of our houses was heard to shout 'Get in here for your bath, school tomorrow'

*

Bob saw it first lying in the long grass where somebody too lazy to take it to the tip or burn it (too big) had dumped it. A wide pine, splinter covered fencing panel, it would make a great roof for the fort we had just (coincidentally) thought about building. Barry and I took one end, Bob, Kevin and Les the other (this was man's work). Serena, Sandra and Gillian (Barry's sister) walked ahead looking out for land mines, bear traps and snakes hidden in the rugged terrain and we set off.

We all knew exactly where to take our discarded panel to, where the basics for building it were already conveniently in place, including a deep channel in the earth that ran alongside. We'd used it many times as a lair but it had never been completely waterproof, a drop of rainwater and our lair was a muddy pond.

Between Kevin's back garden and the backfields was a tall sturdy wire fence and directly behind it over the years tall trees had grown giving sparse shelter.. Attempting to get the panel into position was no easy task, the lower branches of the overhanging trees weren't overly pleased by being squashed down, the stinging nettles underneath them closed ranks between our naked knees and the channel miraculously became wider the more we pushed down the panel into a sharper angle.

'It keeps sliding down the fence' said my annoying sister Sandra when we boys had finally manoeuvred the panel into place, she was right of course but still annoying. It needed bedding down into the earth at the bottom to stop it sliding down the fence wire.

So Sandra and Serena stood on the bottom of it at ground level and slowly inched their way up the angled incline forcing it to dig more firmly into the earth. It was then I had the great idea of getting under the panel and…not really sure what my great idea was and what I was going to do once there, but I did it anyway…I stooped down under the panel.

Someone then shouted to Sandra and Serena 'Stamp up and down, that should force it…'

That's all I can remember…my world went black. Apparently the wide wooden panel slid down the fence and with my two lovely sisters still standing on it came down on me and my head. In hindsight I must have been unconscious for no more than a few seconds but my headache lasted the rest of the day. 'Better go home and tell mum' Serena said 'No way!' I replied, as a little dribble of blood dripped down my forehead. We had a fort to build!

*

Banana Splits

We called it the 'Old Barn' probably because it was an old barn. Situated down a long overgrown dirt track, meandering through cow and sheep inhabited fields it was a place we spent many a long day trespassing in.

It had a number of outbuildings which we took to be milking sheds and stables for horses along with pens for chickens and a pig sty. Why it appeared to have been abandoned we could never or more likely didn't bother to comprehend, it was big and had enormous potential for all sorts of misdemeanours.

Barry suggested a plague had wiped out the previous occupants and their bodies were buried in the fields. Les went for alien abduction, I couldn't care less because when it rained we had lots of places to shelter.

The main part of the barn was two stories high with a thick rope hanging down through a trap door for access to the second floor (for us kids it was an easy arm over arm schimmy with skinny leg support).

To one side of the lower floor was a set of steps obviously for older people's use lay smashed and broken on the ground.

Once we were up the rope and standing on the rotten floorboards of the upper floor we were safe from prying adults and armed police.

From there it was easy to climb out and onto the roof which was covered with large grey slates most of which were loose.

Many a time a loose slate would become dislodged from under a size five bumper boot covered foot and go sliding earthwards leaving the unfortunate climee scrabbling for finger holds on hopefully securer slate.

No-one actually fell off the roof which was a pity really, what a story that would have made back at school?'

Once on the roof the view was great, unobscured to the river one way and to the main road (which was miles away) the other. We'd sit up there for hours (which in kids terms probably meant minutes), sucking the chocolate off Rolos and with chocolate coloured spit, having spitting contests the grey slates a good marker making it easy to measure spit distances due to the spit splats.

Apart from sweets us Cecs had a healthy and varied diet when out roaming the countryside of Reading, for energy we'd consume plenty of swiss rolls, they were dirt cheap and came in various flavours and for balance we'd add a savoury snack of Ritz cheese crackers or Quavers depending on funds, all this we'd wash down with Corona Cream soda or Coke, Corona favoured because after consumption we could get threepence back on the bottle or use said bottle for catapult practice.

It was after such a beano that we first heard the sounds of the beast.

We were all sitting on the first floor of the barn having climbed up the rope and pulled it up after us (high tech security) and the inhuman baying chilled us to the bones.

From the ground beneath us came a ferocious din made obviously by a ferocious animal that had only one thing on its rabid mind, to drag us all down to its lair and strip the skin from bodies. Its demonic growling reverberated in the hollow barn and bounced off the wooden walls echoing and amplifying to such an extent that we could almost feel it. We all sat as still as possible, arms wrapped around our knees, eyes like dinner plates staring at each other and swallowing hard.

Now the beast from below was leaping backwards and forwards, its paws digging huge clumps from the ground, saliva dripping from its teeth filled jaws as it circled in tight frenzied bounds.

We could not see anything of this of course but we could hear the noises and our imaginations did the rest.

One of us had to do it and because David was the smallest and easiest to beat up if he wouldn't, the job fell to him, we further encouraged him by pointing to the trap door and waving clenched fists at him.

After many useless pleading looks David got down on to his belly and started to crawl towards the secured part of the hanging rope.

Having reached the lip of the trap door he slowly lifted his head and peered over and into the gloomy abyss.

'It's a huge wolf and it's leaping up the walls trying to get at us, and when it does it's going to eat us' He screamed hysterically and scuttled back to his place on the floor, hands over his crotch.

We all exchanged terrified glances and backed away from the gaping trapdoor on our bums.

We were all going to die, the wolf was calling to its mates, we could all hear it in its howls, in its wolf's language.

Silence, a sudden silence, as one we all stared in abject horror at the opening that was the trap door, any second now the huge animal's head was going to…

'Ellie, come here you naughty girl, Ellie come here at once'

The voice was that of an angel and all at once we let go of our crotches.

'Its alright' said the voice of the angel, you can come down Ellie won't hurt you'

We climbed down the rope one by one and one by one on reaching the ground were covered in muddy paws and copious amounts of dog spittle.

*

'You're a girl Sandra what do you like the smell of?' We had spent ages going through the bins collecting glass bottles of all shapes and sizes.
We found little plastic funnels, tupperware mixing jugs and a whisk from Barry's mum's kitchen cupboards. We even discovered small circular filter papers from somewhere in the back of one of the cabinets fixed to the wall. We were now ready to make our own perfume,(Sandra insisted on calling it a scent, much posher she said) by bottling it, taking it around the streets of Southcote and making our fortune.
The search for ingredients had begun.
Outside our front door grew two large lavender plants, they would be a start, they smelt really perfurminy…we pulled huge bits off and put them in the mixing tubs and covered it all with water. We stank of lavender for ages, it left its powdery stuff all over us.
Next we needed something a bit sweeter, something that didn't stink of lavender, flowers. (Sandra had suggested that), We went around peoples gardens

pulling up anything flower looking. All this was put into our mixing tubs and mashed together.

And now to add our magic ingredient, vinegar and to this day I have never been able to answer the question asked by so many Why? I think it might have something to do with its fumey quality and how nice it tasted on chips.

Never in the field of perfume making was so much effort put in for so many and sold to so few..

Yes, we added vinegar.

Barry suggested boiling it all, if we did think it wouldn't do any good we didn't voice it because boiling it sounded like great fun and was obviously very professional (Les said that). The vessel we decided on to pour our mulchy mixture in was an old empty paint tin (plenty of these in sheds all over the estate) and let's face it paint does smell a bit perfumy doesn't it?

We built a mini bonfire in Barry's back garden (which was also filled with enough rubbish and wood to burn) and borrowing the silver rack from his mums grill pan (she was out) laid it over a couple of bricks (also available from sheds all over the estate) over the mini bonfire and we were ready to boil away.

We lit the fire and with the aid of a little splosh or two of methylated spirits (kept in the shed for Barry's elder brother Malcolms static steam engine). We soon had a good little blaze going with sticks to prod and encourage it. With the mixed aroma's of paint, vinegar, meths and burning wood wafting around us our original idea of making perfume drifted away with the darkening smoke. The licking flames and bubbling goo in the tin was mesmerising, we felt the warmth on our bare knees and took it in turns to get more fuel to fuel the fire.

I think it was Barry's dad or his uncle Dave that rushed out of the back door with the washing up bowl full of cold water but whoever it was wasted no time in throwing it all over our-man made volcano and he wasn't too fussy as to how much he threw over us. Our dream of *The Scent of Southcote Estate,* London, Paris and Rome never quite made it outside of Barry's back garden.

*

'It's been adopted to me' Les told me as we hurried along the country lane on our bikes 'It's name is Ginger'

Eventually we reached a five bar gate, leant our bikes against it and sat astride the top of it. 'There he is' Les said, pointing a finger at a lone ginger coloured horse in the field busy eating grass and swatting flies with its tail.

'Watch' said Les. He climbed down the gate, bent over and tugged a huge handful of long grass from the ground and waving it in the air shouted 'Ginger, come here boy' The horse remained where it was, in the field eating grass and swatting flies with its tail.

'Maybe if you did it as well' Les said, bending over to pick me a huge handful of long grass from the ground.

He climbed back up the gate, handed me the long grass and we both shouted 'Ginger, come here boy' The horse remained where it was in the field eating grass and swatting flies with its tail.

'Shall we go in and..?'

Les must have seen the look on my face because he didn't say any more.

We started to climb down the gate when all of a sudden I saw Ginger raise his head and to my delight start to walk towards us, Les followed my eyes so we both climbed back up the gate again, we had Ginger's attention.

'See, I told you' he said.

It seemed to take an age, Ginger was an old horse and in no hurry to go anywhere. Eventually he came to within a few feet of us and was tempted to come even closer when we offered him the grass.

'Keep your hand flat or he will bite your fingers off' Les said.

And then we heard it, a motor bike coming towards us from somewhere down the lane. Les and I turned to look at each other with the same thought, we could still hear the bike's engine but it wasn't coming into view. Ginger had stopped eating his grass as if he was hearing it as well.

Then we noticed that Ginger had his tail high in the air and I swear he was smiling, not only was he smiling he was farting. Les's horse Ginger was farting, the motor bike would never appear because it wasn't its engine making the noise it was Ginger passing wind, a lot of wind, clouds of it.

It had to stop soon, the passing of wind, but no it just kept on coming. Les looked at me, I looked at Les and all the time we were looking at each other the fart carried on. I don't know who fell off the gate first, maybe we fell off it together but when we hit the ground and were rolling about holding our stomachs and laughing the fart carried on its merry way. With every gasping breath we took and with tears coursing down our cheeks we pleaded with Ginger to stop but it was plain to hear Ginger had no intention of calling an end to his endless passing of wind.

He did eventually of course but we had to walk our bikes the first few yards back down the lane our legs were far too wobbly to pedal.

*

The Jetsons

British Bulldog, or a Cecs version of it played in the middle of the road on a warm summer's night. I'd always thought the name was silly and we made it up but if you've got the time (or already got bored with my ramblings and desperately wanting to do something else, look it up)...We took the concept of the game and this is what we did with it.

Someone was designated the Bulldog, he/she had to stand a short distance away from the group of us remaining and wait. One of us in the group would throw the ball as high into the air as he/she could (if we still had a ball amongst us that wasn't lost somewhere already in a neighbours garden, a tin can would do).

Now forgive me my dear fellow Cecs but I may have a few details a bit askew here but please take my great age and the fact of my developing senility into account as you read on.

As the ball/can was airbourne the group walked as swiftly away from the Bulldog standing waiting to catch it as possible. It was not allowed to go into any neighbours gardens (who were probably huddled in front of their black and white televisions watching 'The Saint' or something on one of the other two channels, wishing that the noisy brats would go indoors or it would start raining).

Once the Bulldog had successfully caught the ball/can he/she would shout out 'British Bulldog' as loud as they could.

On hearing this each member of the group had to on pain of death stop where exactly they were and go no further.

Now it was the Bulldogs prerogative to select a group member (if you were a boy it was usually the furthest one away then you could show off your muscles and your aim.

The Bull Dog could then take a number of steps (agreed on before the game commenced) and throw the ball as hard as he/she could at her desired target. The said target was not allowed to move at all so a shot at his/hers face was always the most satisfying one especially if it was accurate.

If he/she hit the target he/she became the next Bulldog and the whole thing would start again and continue until too many Cecs grew fed up with hopping from one leg to the other and had to go indoors for a long satisfying wee.

*

'Have you seen Graham, wow, you should see Graham?'

It was Kevin, he lived in posh Worcester Close and he was bursting with excitement.

Graham lived around the corner in Worcester Close as well, not far enough to take our bikes so we walked.

Barry and I wondered what was wrong with Graham, hopefully nothing too trivial, for a Cec Graham was a bit posh and a bit stuck up, living in posh Worcester Close and all.

Barry knocked on the door and a lady with high hair answered.

'Have you seen my Graham?' she said and without waiting for a reply she turned her head and (not sounding the least bit Worcester Close) shouted 'Graham'. And then leaving the front door open she disappeared back into the house that was smelling strongly of Pledge.

After a while Graham appeared at the door, both of his hands clasped tightly over his nose, mouth and chin.

'What do you want?'

His voice sounded odd but it always did as he was a little bit posh.

'Are you alright?' Barry asked, more out of burning curiosity than care.

It was then that Graham lowered his hands and both Barry and I took an immediate and involuntary step backwards.

Both of Graham's eyes were blackened, dark shadows of bruising ran down the sides of his nose, his lips were red and puffed out and there was a cut to his chin in the early stages of scabbing'

'What happened to you?' I'd asked the question before remembering to add a sympathetic tone to my voice.

Graham began to speak but you could hear the pain it caused him.

'You know that aluminium catapult with the thick black elastic I bought at the Army and Navy store? (I told you he was posh) I tried it out down the Holy Brook yesterday' He paused to wipe a posh tear from his cheek, I stared at Barry in awe as to what was coming next.

'Well, I let go of the wrong end' said Graham as he shut the door in our faces.

Barry and I sobbed with laughter the entire walk back down posh Worcester Close.

*

Mrs. Haines had acquired a new fridge, probably on the never never mum said. It was delivered in a huge cardboard box by a man on a sack truck. Gillian, her daughter, was standing in the doorway in everyone's way.

'Can I have the empty box mum?' she was saying over and over again.

'Bloody 'ell Gillian, let the man get the bloody thing through the door first will you?'

Gillian had had a brilliant idea looking at the shape of the big box, in her eyes it would make a great Punch and Judy Hut and she herself would make a great Punch and Judy being the budding actress that she was.

The fridge finally found itself in the kitchen, unboxed and plugged in and being fed with foodstuff. Gillian found herself outside in the back garden surrounded by packing innards and the object of her desires: the now empty cardboard box..

With a pair of scissors, a few crayons and some of Barry's model aeroplane paint for the finer details she soon had the hut made, decorated and standing proud in the back garden steadied by guy ropes from an old tent holding it in position. It looked just like the one on Littlehampton beach with enough room inside to put the kitchen chair in for props to be stored on.

She took some of her dolls from her bedroom downstairs and set the hut up in her back garden Punch and Judy show (of sorts) ready for the showing.

Gillian was older and cleverer than us kids so when she invited us to watch her show we all jumped at the invitation.

It was a very hot day and we sat on makeshift seats, mine being an upside down plastic bucket, my skinny knees sticking out from my shorts, drinking homemade cloudy lemonade and eating plain crisps sprinkled with oxo cubes.

Only minutes into the show and the whole ensemble erupted into hysterical laughter, Gillian had put down her dolls and was pointing at me with one hand and covering her mouth with the other. My knees were not the only things sticking out of the bottom of my shorts.

I looked down in horror and found that because of the angle I was sitting on the plastic bucket my willy was poking its head out as well.

*

The Flintstones

As afternoon drifted into evening we loved to play games or use toys out on the street, British bulldog, tin can alley, rounders, cricket using the lamp post as wickets, its lamp as floodlights, foot tennis using the tar strips in the road as a net and allowing the ball only one bounce per square - tig, kiss chase and along the grass verges, conkers, marbles and leaning cigarette cards up against the wall and flicking others then to knock them down. How about knocking on doors and running away, that really annoyed people. We'd fly balsa wood planes, speed up and down the pavement on scooters, and homemade trolleys.

For the girls, never for the boys (I'm not being sexist, sexism wasn't invented then, not on the Southcote Estate at least and the first time (not last) I was called a chauvinist pig I replied indignantly, no I'm not I'm C of E) skipping, hopscotch, cat's cradle with wool, five stones with little metal star shaped things, hula hoops, roller skating, three balls bounced against a wall whilst singing little rhymes, catch and many more.

*

Seasons came and seasons went but nobody on our council estate could tell you when the marble season would be upon us, it just was and when it was the roads were busy either side by all manner of marbles and marblers.
Out came bags of marbles, no-one knew where they had been up until then and after a period of frantic marbling the marbles disappeared back into their little bags.
All sizes of marbles had all sorts of names, the bigger Smashers, Giants, Thumpers, Bonkers and Toebreakers, the smaller Brooklyn Dodgers and Pee Wees, us Cecs simplified it, we had Alleys or Allies and half Allies and if you were really lucky you might own a ball bearing, I did and it was big and weighed half a ton. A twentier at least! I'll explain.
Along the side of the roads were grass verges, these verges created little shallow gullies where grass met concrete, long and narrow these gullies were ideal for rolling your marble along.

After choosing which marble he was going to use, the one who went first rolled his marble using thumb and forefinger, along said gully. The second player rolled his marble after it, if he hit it he could claim it if not the first player went again and had the opportunity of 'going for' the first marble rolled..either backwards or forward depending where it ceased rolling..with me ? Now to complicate it if it wasn't complicated the first time - if the first player to roll his marble had chosen an Alley or a half Alley opposed to a Pee Wee that particular marble would need to be hit 4 times if it were an Alley or only twice if it were a half Alley, and of course only once it being a Pee Wee. It goes without saying but I'm going to say before going, this made life harder for the hitter rather than the hittee because glass marbles have a unique way of bouncing off each other and the hitting marble could and did fly off anywhere. The secret being in which size marble does the first marbler choose.

P.S. My ball bearing came from a train's wheel and would've taken 20 hits to win it, if I ever played it, which I didn't, I didn't want to lose it.

*

If it was the right time of the year all you needed was a good stout stick, a strong throwing technique and of course a well endowed Horse Chestnut tree, two of which were in abundance in Prospect Park. The harder and higher you threw your stick into the tree branches one of two things was probably going to be the result.

1) You were showered by little vivid green spiky and spiteful hand grenades called conkers or 2) You lost your stick. 'Careful where you throw your stick' I shouted at Les, 'They don't grow on trees you know' Collecting the conkers that no longer grew on the trees but were scattered all over the grass was a finger spiking job!

Preparing the little vivid green, spiky spiteful hand grenades was best done in situ as putting them in your pocket to take home was a definite no no. Relieving the conkers of their outer shells was best done by cracking them underfoot and prising your prize out with your fingers and what a prize they were?

Whoever thought of pushing a skewer right through the centre of them, threading string through the hole and securing the string in a tight knot at one end (after soaking them overnight in vinegar to harden as we Cecs did) then swinging them viciously in downward whiplike strokes in an effort to smash one against the other and then shout 'whoopee' as your opponents conkers brains flew out in all directions surely never took the time to gaze at the sheer beauty of their highly polished brown silky patterned surfaces.

*

Rocky and his friends

The activity known as Knuckles was for the far more sadistic and macho of us Cecs. It was an activity that required a lot of strength, acumen, speed, accuracy and very little brain, therefore I would often participate in it with my little sisters, for practice or a fruit gum.
Standing a step apart and facing each other you place your closed fist against your opponent's, knuckle to knuckle.
On the word 'go' you apply forward pressure and hold it staring into each other's eyes and without showing it wish you were somewhere else. After a decent amount of dramatic interlude you steel yourself for the pain you could, if not quick enough, receive. With as fast a movement of your arm as you can achieve you snatch away your fist and raise it, if your opponent has not been as quick as you in retrieving his/hers proffered knuckles you slam your knuckles down on said opponents as hard as you can.
Bone against bone makes a disturbing noise.
'Ouch that hurt' or words to effect he/she will probably say as you turn to receive your well deserved applause from the baying audience.

*

Essential items required on any Council Estate…
Water pistol, spud gun, catapult, pea shooter, pea
gun, cap gun, (mine was a silver 'Pony Boy' cap gun,
it held rolls of caps and fired them one at a time)
sticks, plastic swords, gat gun, bow and arrow, pea
gun, boomerang, lasso, kites, spinning tops and
those plastic rocket shaped things you put caps in
and threw up in the air, gyroscopes that when spun
with tight string balanced themselves on the tip of
pencils.

And then one of the most nerve wracking, knee
scraping spectator escapades…hurtling towards a
bending corner in the road on your bike and with
expert, or sometimes not so expert timing, and at top
speed slamming your pedal backwards and grinding
it hard against the kerbstones surface…if you were
lucky you'd send a flurry of sparks into the night sky
and listen to kids go 'Wow, yeah, look at all those
stars', unlucky you'd end up in a tangled mess on the
road with a mudguard as a scarf.

*

Downtown - Petula Clark

It was written for me. I would sit on the upper deck of the double decker bus (in the front looking out of the window if I was lucky) my half a crown clenched in my fist (ten bob note if I was lucky) on my way downtown, humming it to myself.

I was never alone really being surrounded by people of course and my only worry was that my catapult elastic was beginning to fray, but that didn't matter and the noise and hurry excited me. It was invigorating.

Reading was downtown, downtown was Reading to us Cecs.

The bus fare, (thrupence one way), I would get from having previously taken back a corona bottle to the shops (I'd find one somewhere) thusly I would not to break into my half a crown or ten bob note before starting my journey (downtown) The return journey I usually walked if all my funds had been exhausted (downtown).

He was a short grey haired man and he spoke with a high pitched voice.

'Fares please, move along the bus, hold tight, Frilsham Road next stop, and then the bus conductor in the black suit and peaked cap would be standing next to me, a worn leather money bag strapped across one shoulder and a ticket machine the size of Jodrell bank the other.

We'd pass the big church at the bottom of Castle Hill where I once asked my Dad..'Why are the doors to that church so big?' And he replied without missing a beat 'So the elephants can get in'
The Butts, St.Marys Butts, I could get off here or go through to Broad Street or sometimes Reading General Station, the world was my oyster, I was a free spirit.
What shop first?' The Dolls Hospital ?' A strange name for a toy shop but it held for me a multitude of goodies (and hopefully some catapult elastic).
Maybe Rumbelows next or Hickies where you could ask to listen to a record and nestle in a converted egg box and listen to it, if you had time, an L.P. (a big record with more records on it).
When I felt energetic and felt like a bit of a walk, Walls Carnival Stores would be my next port of call, where everything had been waiting for me, downtown.

When I wasn't going downtown, everything waiting for me, I would be on the same bus with my mum going to visit my Auntie Joan.
The bus would go into the town through the parts familiar to me and then begin its journey the other side of Reading to Caversham and yonder parts foreign.

Did the conductor send secret messages to the driver when he rang the bell, or was there a hole through to his cab where he spoke to him directly?
Either way I could never understand how the driver knew exactly where my Auntie Joan lived, he didn't ask my mum and he certainly never asked me.
Strange then that everytime we went to visit Auntie Joan, who lived a long way away the driver always knew exactly where she lived and always stopped right outside her house.
The fact that that was the bus terminal never entered my head, not for an embarrassingly long time.

*

Camberwick Green

Where the A4 and Southcote Lane meet near the Southcote Hotel and lying back from both roads behind a number of trees was the Haunted House.
The name we Cecs christened it was half right because it wasn't a normal house but it was definitely haunted, ask any one of us, we'll tell you.
It was a huge building with three floors, numerous rooms (which we had explored en masse, too scary to do it alone at first) and linking corridors on all three storeys.
It had a bathroom on each floor and on the ground floor a large reception hall. It also boasted its own

wood and glass conservatory built on one side and what every respectable Haunted House should have, a deep dark cellar. But more importantly than all this, much more, it was empty, full of large areas of emptiness, just shadows and void of having anything in it apart from of course us Cecs occasionally and ghosts permanently.

It was also set a good distance from the main road and only accessible by a gravel drive overgrown with trees and bushes. If all us Cecs were given pen and paper to design a building with as much potential for the sort of things we Cecs have potential to do we could not possibly come up with anything better.

We spent many a happy hour being scared to death in it but never dared to go it alone, this was our way of establishing that we all got scared to death satisfactorily and had our own tales to tell.

And then our initiation test, to make men out of boys, devised by the most sadistic of our number, me.

We had to take it in turns, my rules were strict and had to be obeyed or the chosen victim would be unmercifully teased for as long as we could keep it up.

Starting from the reception hall at the front of the building we all had to take it in turns to carry out the 'Dash of Death' and because it was my idea I deemed myself to go first and since deeming myself, was already regretting it.

Holding three emptied coke cans I had to dash up the staircase right to the third floor and once there place one of the cans on the top step. Then with two cans left I had to dash along the corridor to the other end of the building and place a second can on the top step of the downward staircase.

Having done that I had to dash down those steps and place the last can on the floor before dashing back the way I'd come, leaving the cans in situ as proof of my compliance to the rules,my own rules..

Of course if I was lucky enough to get back to the awaiting Cecs without getting my throat cut or having my lifeblood sucked from my veins the next Cec had to go and collect cans proving he had done the deed as well. Easy.

I was well up the very first two steps when fear took over from what little common sense I had, standing above me wearing clothes straight out of a Charles Dickens novel stood a shadow. I took another two steps up (due to my forced forward motion more than anything else) and the shadow became a properly formed shadow before disappearing into the shadows.

And I'd only just started, I was still in view of my fellow Cec's standing below me at floor level, I could not afford them seeing any further hesitation on my part, so heart thumping under my woollen sleeveless jumper I pushed myself onward towards whatever fateful fate awaited me.

I was at the top of the stairs, the third floor, the echoes of my footfalls following me, chasing me. I bent to place the first can down on the top step and tried desperately not to look to my right and down the corridor I knew to be there stretching for what seemed miles in front of me. Now out of sight from my fellow Cecs the urge to turn back, run back and say 'Who's stupid idea was this?' was almost overwhelming. But blind panic took me forward, passing one room after another, one doorway after another, some open wide, some ajar, some closed completely, all insisting that I stop my foolish attempts to escape them and to enter them. It had been my plan not to run but my legs were obviously not in with my plan because despite me they were running which only fueled my fear further.

I'm not sure whether running made the experience better or worse because the thought of running into some hidden evil being or being chased by one is about equally as bad as it gets. I decided to walk, albeit very fast.

Don't look in the rooms Kim, keep your eyes looking ahead, you don't need to look in the rooms Kim, no point looking into the rooms Kim, ignore them, if you don't look you won't see anything, not that there's anything to see of course, what do you expect to see, nothing if you don't look, maybe something if you do.

I looked into every room it was impossible not to.

I reached the second landing a few seconds before the echoes of my footfalls reached me and placed the empty can down, with no preamble I started to descend the second flight of stairs.

Gripping the third and last can in my white knuckled fist and wondering that if I threw it hard enough would it land where I hoped it would land and save me the terror of taking it down myself. Not a chance was the disappointing thought that came back to me.

After what seemed an age of hurtling down the steep bare floorboards of dusty steps I finally made it to the ground floor and put the last can down.

The feeling of elation in me was transient (strangely enough, the title of a book I was to write years later) as I realised that what I had just experienced I would have to experience all over again only in reverse.

But why should the thought of having to go back the way I had just been have bothered me at all? I'd already stepped every step,crossed every floorboard and looked in every room with no problems…it didn't quite work like that..

I started back up the steps in the firm knowledge that all would be fine..and got at least three steps up before the fears won me over again, the ghouls, ghosts and evil presences had watched me go by the first time and had had time to prepare themselves for the event of my return. I had played right into their claws.

I will save you the details of my return journey through hell dear reader, suffice to say I didn't enjoy it a great deal (I had a good few nightmares about it for the following weeks) but I will try to pass on the feelings of wicked enjoyment I got back safely and looked into the eyes of the next boy who had to follow me and then whispered in his ear.
'When you get up to the third floor be careful when passing the fourth door on your left'

*

Jonny Quest

A bridge, a brick built bridge spanning the Holy Brook and carrying the Burghfield Road on its back, *(I have no idea if that is its real name, Holy Brook, I could look it up but to me and others it would always be called the Holy Brook, after all you don't change your old friends names as you get older do you?)*
It was a bridge like no other, it was an arch over a bigger arch which meant the space between the two arches was hollow. So by taking a careful step into a well trodden hole in the crumbling brickwork and a twist of your body over the water below you could hoist yourself into said hollow.
'Kim loves Carol 'was etched high into its arching roof many years ago and I have no doubt it is still there! But back to the bridge, the monument that is still so vivid in my mind I can walk upon its brick floor from

edge to edge and listen to my own footsteps echoing in its shadowed shelter from the sun and rain.

A great place to eat your peanut butter sandwiches, drink your Corona fizzy orange from the bottle and squat and tie a bent pin on the end of your fishing line.

A great place to sit and wait for your trousers to dry after a swim in the brooks cold, clear waters.

A great place to light a bonfire and pretend you were hunters arriving back to your cave after killing a buffalo.

A great place to practise skimming the water with a stone and seeing how many leaps you can achieve.

A great place to snog with Carol.

And a great place to practise your Dead Man's Fart technique, dead man's fart I hear you say? I will enlighten you.

Select a nice flat stone with a bit of weight to it. Hold it vertically in your hooked index finger and lob it as high in the air as you can, giving it rapid flicking spin as you open your digit as you launch it into the sky. If you've got your aim and trajectory right the stone should reach a fair height spinning all the time and then start to descend down into the water where with a satisfying 'pphhhuuuttt' it enters at speed, sending up an explosion of tiny rippling bubbles of foam in its wake. Your dead man's fart is judged by the amount of laughter it receives from its audience standing on the banks.

*

We called them Rail Cars, they were green square shaped trains that although being called trains did a lousy job at being trains. They were slow, clumsy-looking and rocked from side to side if they ran over anything bigger than a penny (which had previously been put on the rail by us of course to be flattened by tons of the said train) a sort of by-product of what was the main agenda to prevent us getting bored!. A game called Suicide and the clue was in its name. Me, Les, Mark, Barry, Steve and Dave and my brother Bob were all standing on the railway bridge that spanned the Holy Brook awaiting the train's snail-like approach.

Wearing short trousers, sandals and with our shirts hanging on a nearby tree we must have put the fear of God into the poor driver as he neared us and watched as we climbed up the iron bridges greased and coal dust covered skeletal structure.

'Where the hell are those little brats going, and why? Through the dirty windows of his cab and silhouetted now again against flashes of sun the poor driver must have thought we looked like a row of moving black charred trees in the aftermath of a nuclear explosion. At the last few seconds just as the train closed the distance between us and it, with a thumbs up signal, we all jumped as one, screaming loudly like

Banshees through the wide gap between the bridge and rails into the freezing waters of the Holy Brook far below us.

It was a few days later and we were having tea. Dad was reading an article in the Reading Evening News and grunting every now and again.
'Well, I'd skin the silly little buggers alive if I ever caught them doing anything as bloody stupid as this' He was jabbing angrily at the opened page with his right index finger and pushing it out towards us inviting us to read it.
Bob and I were studying the pattern on the tablecloth as if we'd never seen it before.

*

Bowling underhand seemed to cure it. Bob (elder brother) found it hard to hit the ball if I bowled over hand because the back garden was small and space limited.

Sandra, (oldest sister) fielded in dad's freshly dug over cabbage patch, Serena (middle sister) fielded further away at the back of the garden next to the tall wire fence, dodging the stinging nettles as best she could and (Jackie youngest sister) sat on the grass busy making daisy chains.

We had searched every cupboard in the house for a cricket ball, a tennis ball, or a dogs ball (the latter being a bit of a long shot seeing as we didn't even have a dog) but the only round object we found was a golf ball, it would have to do.

Again I found myself bowling and aiming at the white wickets chalked heavily on the brick wall of the back of the house, again my brother hit the golf ball too hard and again it flew over the low fence and landed in a patch of unruly weeds in Mrs Haines garden.

I surprised myself by coming out with swear words I had never heard before.

Sandra stood rooted to the spot amongst the cabbages (see what I did there?)' Serena thought about moving but was on the wrong side of a large stinging nettle contingent, Jackie was as usual, oblivious to everything.

I was still swearing at my big brother as I clambered over the fence to hopefully retrieve the ball from the dense vegetation that had appeared to have swallowed it.

My female siblings all at once looked at me for some sort of guidance.

'Six' shouted my smirking brother.

It was carryinging on playing cricket or going inside to watch Saturday Wrestling..and the football results, we all chose the former and took up our positions, I had two bowls left in my over.

When my dear brother hit my next bowl and sent it to land inches from whence I had just previously retrieved it something came adrift in my head.

I leapt over the low fence as if it wasn't there, snatched the ball from its would be hiding place, pirouetted like Nijinsky and threw the tiny ball with all my might straight at Bob's unprotected head.

He ducked. The ball went straight through the window behind him leaving a perfect circular hole and Dunlop 3 imprinted on the glass's smooth edge.

Five kids with mouths the same shape as the hole in the window, only much bigger, stood in terrified silence..Dad would kill me and they probably wouldn't get their 'plate of things*' before bed that night.

It was time for me not to be there.

I ran in the back door, (Dad was busy staring at the new ventilation in the window, mum was picking up the golf ball looking at Dad and I was tearing through the lounge (front room) on my way to the stairs and the (I was well aware, temporary sanctuary of my bedroom).

Having reached it unscathed I slammed the door, locked it and for good measure stuck my duffle bag at its base.

I lay on my bed listening to the furore downstairs and crying, somehow I had managed to fall asleep deep under the heavy cover of my eiderdown knowing nothing of what transpired in the meantime…

Luckily dad had realised he was late for the pub and a few bits of sellotape would sort out the window tomorrow, but with a bit of good fortune mum would sort it all out.

Having tried to open my bedroom door and banging hard on it Mum was left with only one recourse.

Tom Brown, the man who drove the big red tipper lorry and lived almost opposite us was summoned. Muscled and grimy Tom was called on for all manner of jobs that needed doing on the estate. Tom had a ladder, Tom had drain clearing rods, Tom had heavy duty bolt cutters, Tom had an angle grinder, Tom could weld, Tom could rewire an entire electric sub station with a teaspoon, Tom could go faster than a speeding train, Tom was more powerful than a locomotive, Tom could leap over tall buildings at a single bound. I learnt later that someone called Thomas Hughes even wrote a book about the amazing Tom Brown. It was called Tom Brown's Schooldays, but Tom was a bit of a show off if you ask me.

Tom had a ladder (as previously stated in his list of extensive qualifications) and standing on top of this ladder and staring in through the window of my bedroom, Tom gave me the fright of my life.

* A plate of things consisted of an apple, a piece of cheese, crisps and maybe a couple of biscuits if we were in the money that week.

The Christmas tree lights would not do as their name implied, light.

Tom Brown had been summoned. Mum let him in as Dad was leaving for the pub, a strong smell of Brylcreem and Golden Virginia in his wake. I had left my sanctuary, the coast now being clear.

Tom Brown armed with a screwdriver and a pair of pliers went straight to the light plug and socket in the wall. Checking for blown fuses he found nothing untoward he put the plug back in its socket and turned his attention to the small sealed plastic switch box fitted to the lights flex.

I was sitting on the sofa watching Stingray on the telly and wondering what could happen in the next half hour.

Tom had taken the little box from the lights and was gently poking his screwdriver into it.

It was then that I was overcome with inspiration when I noticed that although the plug to the lights was snuggly fitted into the socket the mains switch was up.

I would show (know it all) Tom Brown how clever he was..I got up from the sofa and without him seeing I reached for the switch and pushed it down.

Tom Brown immediately began to sing a strange high pitched song and bright sparks flew from the little black box. His screwdriver embedded itself into our artexed ceiling and Tom Brown did a little dance to accompany his singing.
Mum went out and bought some new lights.

*

Old man Sid (Les's dad) would leave us at the Esso garage on the Bath Road from 6pm to about 10.30pm and we would man the petrol pumps to earn extra pocket money. Although we came home reeking of petrol, we loved the job and earned more than we were actually paid, let me explain…(and it would help you to be reminded that tills in those days were wooden contraptions that printed out a minimum of info).
If a customer asked for over a certain amount of fuel we had to knock a shilling off the cost for them.
By putting aside all the money paid for the fuel that was under the qualifying amount and not putting it in the till until it had exceeded the target, we were (as far as we were concerned) the legal owners of the shilling.
After many months it was discovered that when Les and I looked after the garage that no customer ever

bought less fuel than was required to qualify for the shilling off. How weird is that ?

When a television star by the name of Tommy Trinder turned into our garage all our birthdays came at once. After spending twenty minutes trying to find out how to open the fuel cap on the Rolls (a button on the dashboard) we were asked to 'Fill 'er up' at an eye watering cost. Not only did we acquire a few shillings because we forgot (as we were highly skilled in doing) to tell him about the savings, we were also told to keep the change.

Assorted Bon Bons,crisps and cans of pepsi all around.

The big black Mercedes 200D housed behind the up and over doors in another part of the garage finally became less of a mystery and more of an attraction, one we could ignore for no longer.

Although Les and I were informed that if we even so much as touched it we would probably never be able to father children when we were older the temptation for the attraction blossomed.

The front of the beast was barely inches from the steel doors, its red and white temporary number plate virtually touching it, the back just as close to the back wall of the building. The vehicle was not only unlocked but keys bearing the Mercedes logo were hanging on a hook on an adjacent wall.

'I just want to hear what it sounds like' said Les, (taking down the keys) ' and tell Colin (his brother) 'I almost drove a Mercedes'

Pausing to look all around the small area Les opened the door and sat behind the car's steering wheel, with the key in his right hand, he searched the dashboard for somewhere to put it.

I stood in the open doorway watching him and praying that the owner of the car was eating fish and chips on holiday somewhere like Hayling Island.

And then with an ear splitting roar that bounced off the walls of the small building the car's 2ltr, 4 cylinder engine burst into life. The car sprang forward, stalled, stopped, went as silent as the grave and I was coughing out diesel fumes. For a while it was the silence that was bouncing off the walls and then the soft guilty sound of Les opening the driver side door and stepping out.

We just stood and stared at each other over the black shiny roof of the car both fighting the urge to go up to the up and over doors and therefore able to see what we didn't really want to see, namely the damage we had done to a Mercedes 200D. I started off first being careful not to put my sweaty hands on the car's glossy paintwork, which was ironic really seeing as the front of it was probably wearing the crumpled remains of the up and over garage door.

'Oh my God' Those three words I uttered had Les rooted to the spot at the car's side, his face was as white as the car's leather interior and his eyes as big as its headlights.

Apart from a slight bulging to the bottom of the up and over doors, which a few well aimed kicks from four sized 6 school shoes soon put right and a cracked trade plate the car looked completely unscathed.

'It must have stalled just at the point it hit the door' I said as if I knew what I was talking about, which on that occasion happened to be absolutely right.

And then Les said 'Well it's his fault because he left it in gear'

Vindicated and still a bit shaken we needed two Mars bars pilfered from the garage's cold box to steady our nerves and a quick count of our evening spoils before calling it a night.

*

Yogi Bear

Now I've tied my bent pin (I lied about a bent pin of course, it was a fishing hook really, the bent pin bit sounded far more 'Boys Own') on the end of my line and tired of snogging Beverly, (or the other way round of course) it's time to go fishing.

Armed with a jam jar full of more mud than worms and a pulped mass of
kneaded bread (one I did earlier) me and Barry head upstream to where the water is calm and deep (Here I can imagine the fish spirits come to life from my trilogy 'Return to the Broadwaters' emerging from the murky depths). That's another lie and a blatant plug (I wasn't to pen those books for years to come but I'm sure these waters were to feed my future imaginations).

With a float held in position with bands of rubber and bullets of lead on my line (yes lead, no health and safety in those days) keeping it upright in the waters, Barry and I could sit still and remain quiet for minutes at a time.

And more minutes later I shout from my position a few feet away..

'Barry, you've got a bite'.

My voice bounces from bank to bank and the birds are startled from the trees.

Barry sits up, stops picking his nose, falls backward and as he does so yanks at the rod that up until then had been just lying dormant between his skinny knees. There follows a curious zipping sound and from the water's depth, flying in a high arc over his ducking head, his line, float, weights and wormless hook eventually land in the dense bushes behind him and instantly becomes a tangled mess.

When I finally ceased my laughing and rolling about in the long grass Barry announced he hated tangles and besides 'Lost in Space' started in 25 minutes.

*

The bridge was low above the Holy Brook made of concrete and iron; it was wide enough and easily strong enough to take a tractor, which was what it was probably built for. On one side the brook was an expanse of wild growth through which a gravel lane ran through to Byfield Road on the other side allotments which were completely off bounds to us Cecs, or so the allotmenteers liked to think.
Many times I and other Cecs were chased from this hallowed ground by scythe swinging, green fingered mad men, us dropping carrots and potatoes as we ran. But the main reason for our trespassing was not for vegetables at all, it was for the succulent terrestrial invertebrates that fed on the said vegetables…worms.
With a jam jar full of deep almost black brown earth housing worms the size of anacondas we would retreat to the iron bridge, which incidentally we called the Iron Bridge and a day's fishing would commence. It was a great vantage point to fish from and being low to the water and reinforced underneath with

concrete banks when it rained we could squeeze underneath it all snug and cosy forget about the fish and giggle at naughty books.

This day was warm and sunny, the minnows nipped the surface, the roach teased us in the midstream and the large fat chub idled lazily in the deeper waters under the shade of the banks.

I was lucky I had a blue fibreglass rod (Keith had bought me it but more about him later) and six pound breaking strain line, my fellow Cecs had to do with thin cane or bamboo Woolies rods) that were apt to snap in half if you got your hook caught in a tree.

We had landed a number of small fish enough to make our picnic biscuits taste fishy and our landing net wet.

And then all hell broke loose.

I had been standing on top of one of the bridges raised sides and reeling in my drowned and hook impaled worm when my line abruptly tightened and my rod bent double.

Damn, snagged on a flipping submerged shopping trolley or someone's old weed entangled bike again.

I jumped backwards down onto the bridge's surface just before losing my balance and for a minute thought I was about to go over the exact place I'd been standing leading to an impromptu swim, whilst swinging my rod around and smacking Les across the left side of his face as I did so.

Fighting to stay upright I realised that my rod was going from side to side of the brook and trying its hardest to take me with it.

Somewhere in the darkest recesses of my brain the realisation hit me that I was actually going through the motions of fishing and therefore couldn't it be possible that I might have a big fish on the end of my line.

I became all of a sudden the centre of attraction for my fellow anglers - could it be that Kim has a fish on his line that is bigger than a packet of polos? It was, I did, and I had no idea what to do next, so I did what every inexperienced fisherman does not do when confronted with this dilemma. I dropped my rod and grabbed the line with my bare hands.

To the astounded looks of my fellow anglers I pulled with all of my strength ignoring the questions that were reverberating in my own head 'Why did you do that, why did you drop your rod, isn't fishing exactly what the fishing rod is for?' Blind panic methinks, blind panic at such an age.

Even to this day I wonder why I did, but that's now irrelevant, I did it.

My fellow anglers had laid down their weapons and Barry, (thinking for once like a true angler) went for the landing net that was bone dry and only there for appearances sake, whilst I held on to the jerking line for dear life.

Adrenaline was the only thing now keeping the stinging pain of the ever tightening line (which was now a mini chainsaw) from my hand and from my mind.

This fish was huge in my eyes and tonight it would (along with me) be in a picture on the front page of the Reading Evening News.

After an heroic struggle (by me) that must have gone on for at least three minutes the fish made its first appearance on the surface, flipping its vast tail and drenching us all on the bridge with a white water foaming tsunami (a little bit of the author's poetic licence there!!).

Eventually with the help of my fellow Cecs and a landing net that was full of more bigger holes than smaller we managed to haul the unfortunate fish out of the water and onto the bridge where it flipped about and glared at us.

After a short debate we came to the conclusion that the fish was a chub and must have weighed as much as 3lbs. Considering any fish caught by us prior to this monster did not weigh over 4 oz this indeed was a whale and deserved to be displayed as such.

Using the battered landing net as a stretcher we took the struggling chub to Alan's house in Byfield Road just a few hundred yards away, ran the bath and popped it in.

'Take that bloody thing out, take it to back to the brook and put it back where it belongs' Was what Alan's dad said when we were expecting him to say 'Wow what a beautiful specimen thanks for keeping it to show me it must weigh at least 3 lbs'
We took it back and it was very happy to be returned to its natural world… and no fish were hurt in the telling of this story.

*

It stands proud and majestic in the centre of Prospect Park (which was my second home in Reading, sometimes my first when the old man had been drinking). A huge Regency, Grade 11 listed building called Prospect House, built high upon a grass covered hill. It scowled at passers by and threatened instant death to would be trespassers.
In our day it stood empty and echoey with shadows inside its shadows and wall to wall ghosts.
As legend would have it amongst us 'Cec' dragups a school chum called Danny had one day accidently put his arm through one of its enormous windows and the glass at the top slid down in a guillotine motion severing his arm at his elbow. Not sure if this was true but Danny did have a stump for an arm and it made a really good gory tale for us boys to terrify the girls with and with luck get a quick cuddle, (well we boys thought so anyway).

The back of this huge building had a lower roof which could easily be reached by the footholds on the window ledges and any other brickwork that happened to jut out. Once reaching the top of that lower roof was achieved the rest was just a knuckle grazing shimmy on to the roof proper.

With a leg either side of the apex of the slate covered roof and a practised bum shuffle us kids could go from one chimney to the other spanning the whole building.

The view was incredible and the rusted air raid siren bolted to the side of one of the chimneys brought visions of enemy aircraft flying low over the grass and firing at us, I can still see them now..the bastards.

Les, Steve, Buzzy and I spent hours on the roof of that mansion, no-one could see us and by laying flat on the slates with our bodies draped on one side we could smoke our No.6's drink our Corona orangeade and make faces and unnecessary remarks about the people passing many feet below us who were quite oblivious to us being there.

But the mystery still remains even to this day….

Who spray painted in huge white letters (that could be seen from miles away) right across the mansion's roof the four initials..L.S.B.K.?

Which of course took years to fade away. Les, Steve,Buzzy and I of course had no idea.

*

Sunday afternoons during the school holidays and if the weather was fine you would find half of us Cecs in Prospect Park enjoying the efforts of a group of dedicated people known collectively as the C.S.S.M. the Children's Special Service Mission. These kind people organised games for us Cecs who were in desperate need of being anything near organised. Stretched between two large trees was a banner with the letters C.S.S.M emblazoned on it.

Strange as it may seem but during the morning whilst hymns were being sung and talks about religious matters preached, only a few of us could be found sitting beneath this banner.

In the afternoon when football and cricket were scheduled to be played you couldn't move for us unruly Cecs.. bless you CSSMers folk, you did at least try hard to include us in your 'Character Building Sessions'.

By organising marked off areas in the park with ropes and poles stuck into the grass, and attempting to put us into teams.

We were even given team names i.e. Castle, Abbey, Friary, Minster etc.etc. and play would commence the CSSM's thinking they were in charge and all the time not being in charge at all.

We were a difficult rebellious mob but as I say bless you CSSMers you always persevered.

It was going to one of these gatherings that I witnessed a sight (with others) that has stayed with me all this time. Up in the sky almost directly above us two light aircraft decided to fly the same flightpath, they both did in the end..straight into the ground, both pilots died.

*

The Kennet and Avon Canal is 87 miles long...two lengths of navigable river linked by canal. From Bristol to Bath the river follows the natural course of the River Avon before the canal links it to the river Kennet at Newbury and from there to Reading onto the river Thames.
Before the river gets to Reading it takes a break at least two locations that I'd like to tell to you about, Monkey Island - to pour through a weir to provide various types of amusement and diversions for us Cec's, and a place called Bridge Tree Island - for the sole purpose of providing fun for, Les, Buzzy, David, Mark, and I, but more of that later…

*

Monkey Island, oh Monkey Island, Burghfield, how I and many other Cecs enjoyed your dangerous beauty.

Monkey Island was an Island surrounded by a giant pool of deep angry water fed into it from the River Kennet though a huge weir.

The weir consisted of tall concrete walls and large wooden sluice gates which when opened fully allowed a flow of water to cascade through it which was to us small boys spectacular and just right for diving into.

I looked to my left at the opposite wall as Barry was preparing to hurl himself into the frothing waters, where he would eventually surface would be in the lap of the Gods.

'What are you waiting for cissy?' he screamed up at me a second before he disappeared from sight, maybe forever!

I shut my eyes and despite my brain begging me not to, I dived.

I can still feel the powerful surge of the white water thundering beneath my feet as it forced its way through the concrete weir in swirling eddies. The mighty crash of unstoppable torrents of rushing waves and the pulsating sounds that cancelled out all other sounds, filling my mind with the terrifying promise of a drowning death.

The further the angry white waters carried me from the open mouth of the weir the less turbulent and more calmer it became.

When I managed a quick glimpse of the water below my feet my imagination ran wild. I saw shadows in the murky depths of long lost souls wandering along the weeded bed, their flesh bleached from their bodies, their bones chalk white and brittle and fearsome water dragons indescribable creatures with sharpened gills and pointed teeth.

At last I was in shallow water and the creatures chasing me were back where they belonged in Monkey Island's deepest depths.

Barry was standing on the bank, shivering, laughing and wiping snot from his nose.

'Gotta do that again' he said as he coldly limped back towards the weir's mouth.

'Yeah sure, me too' my traitorous mouth replied.

*

HuckleBerry Hound show

From the Cunning Man pub adjacent to The Peter Pan cafe a narrow lane of well trodden dirt led you along the banks of the Kennet and Avon canal to the glorious sounds and smells of Monkey Island. It was this lane that we were traipsing down for our afternoon swim in its cooling waters, Dad leading his troop of excited children all carrying old towels tightly rolled and stuffed under armpits.

It was a hot still day, the air filled with mayfly, beautifully coloured four winged dragonflies and not to be ignored aggressive wasps, the banks overgrown with huge dock leaves, brambles and warning and heavily armed stinging nettles.

We could smell them long before we saw them, cows gathered in clouds of dust over an empty arid water trough standing and twitching too close together in the heat entrapped behind the barbed wire of a farmers field.

We stopped, we looked, we felt the anguish of the sorry looking cows all with dried tongues and beseeching eyes.

And then dad was galvanised into action. With the hat that once covered his sparse ginger hair he was rapidly walking from the canal to an old redundant enamelled bathroom bath in the opposite field carrying as much water in it as its flimsy sides would permit.

For too long he was fighting a losing battle as the water was being consumed by the thirsty bovines almost before it hit the baths bottom. Dad soldiered on with the sun glaring off his all the time reddening unhatted dome.

*

'Go on then Steve, jump'
We were all there, Monkey Island, us macho boys
treading water in the turbulent currents under the
weir, our outstretched arms holding between us the
huge half inflated inner tube of a recently found
tractor tyre.
'What are you waiting for Steve? Jump !
Steve was standing 15ft above us bare chested,
shivering and pinching his nose between forefinger
and thumb in nervous readiness.
He was to jump off the concrete wall, fly through the
rainbowed mist of spraying water drops and through
the hole in the middle of said inner tube while we all
held it in place on the surface for him.
What could be simpler? We'd all done it previously !!
After what seemed an age of hesitation Steve threw
his pale skinny bones into the air, his legs scissoring,
his arms flailing… 10 ft below shaking water drops
from our eyes, we struggled to keep the innertube in
position on the choppy waters for his entry through it
in the little time we had.
And then an enormous splash, Steve had entered the
big hole in the middle of the innertube, in it, through
it, under it..and the surrounding waters behind him
trailed a slight shade of pink.

Steve swam eagerly to the water's edge and with a
hand on his side staggered onto dry land shouting
and swearing.
We followed dragging the innertube in our wake
curious to see why Steve was acting the way he was.
On closer inspection and to our utter horror we saw
that Steve had a zip like laceration oozing watered
down blood from under his armpit to the top of his
soaked trunks.
On the inner side of the innertube protruded a long
rusted innertube valve, the kind of valve you need to
inflate an innertube.

*

It wasn't too far from Monkey Island but we had never
named it, to us it was just a place to swim when the
hot sun was burning the skin on our backs and arms.
Surrounded by a rusting wire fence adorned every
hundred yards or so by faded and battered signs, we
had no cosy or frivolous name for the gravel pits, they
didn't deserve one.
A huge expanse of steel grey water was surrounded
by dunes of bleached gravel and vast patches of
stinging nettles. Hidden by spiky bramble bushes, a
barbed wire fence supported warning signs (DEEP
WATER KEEP OUT).

We hung our clothes over said signs to keep the insects off them and made our way to the water's edge.

The echoey sounds of splashing feet and laughter smashed the silence as we swam to the one and only outcrop of metal and concrete that broke the water's flat surface at its centre, one hand on it (quickly to avoid its carpet of insects) a quick turn around and back breathlessly to the stones of the shore.

Refreshed after many dives under the surface to be shocked by the sudden drop in temperature and it was time to get out and dry in the heat of the sunshine and make our way home.

Except we didn't all go home, David and Michael wanted more, so we left them to it.

It was only two days later I heard that David had drowned.

We left the gravel pits forever after that, to lie undisturbed beneath its steel grey malevolent surface.

*

Fireball XL5

Large vehicles had to give way to each other going over the old concrete and stone bridge because not only did the Burghfield Road over the river Kennet narrow it also turned a tight curve. Us Cecs were often forced to stop either side to allow a farmer with his herd of cows, a lorry or tractor to pass; if caught half way we would just lay the top of our bodies over the parapet, letting our legs dangle off the road, our bellies pressed against the rounded concrete top and wait.

Get a young boy or a young girl to lay on his/her tummy with his/her feet dangling he/she will laugh, it's a scientific fact, it never fails.

Les, Mark, David, Buzzy and I laughed, the pressure on our bellies threatening a burst of wee from our bladders.

From this unusual angle looking down towards the river we saw something, something we had never seen before, something we would have never seen if we didn't get trapped on the bridge with lorries attempting to traverse both ways at the same time.

An island, well an island of sorts.

Where the river was forced to flow on each side of the bridge's concrete supports and under separate arches a V of mud had slowly developed over the years .

This 'Island' was just big enough to accommodate a couple of tall trees, some bushes and a mud bank, with the river rushing either side of it.

By stretching out as far as you could from the bridge's parapet, saying a little prayer and grabbing at the nearest tree you could wrap your arms and legs around said tree and not fall thirty or so feet into the Kennet's fast flowing current.

From then on it was just a question of leg over arm shimmying until you reached the relative safety of the Islands mud floor.

We had conquered new lands for Queen and Country.

The next thing to do after us intrepid explorers had been intrepid and explored was to name our new kingdom.

All manner of names were suggested as we sat back against the sheer wall of the bridge under the shade of the trees between the fiercely flowing waters but after careful consideration we chose one.

Our new sanctuary existed because of three elements, a bridge, a tree and the island itself.

Swelling with pride and having sworn not to reveal our secret hideaway to another living soul…

especially the Tilehurst Cecs…we named our island 'Bridge Tree Island' and shared a pack of fruit pastilles to celebrate it.

At the pointy end of the triangular island (which was probably no more than fifteen feet from the bridge's shear wall) a large bushy area grew its over hanging branches inches from the fast flowing waters on either side, this is where we made our den.

Room for no more than four at a time no more than four at a time occupied it. Not that we ever expected anybody to even see Bridge Tree Island from the road let alone find their way down to it but what was the use of security if you didn't want to be secure?

Picnics were held on Bridge Tree Island as were fishing contests, archeology digs (digging big holes in the island's mud looking for viking swords).
Vicious wars often occurred between us Cecs and passing, marauding pirate boats where the enemy sniped at us from the poop deck (we called it 'poop deck' because that made us laugh) with peashooters or torpedoed us with imaginary torpedoes. We would return fire with clumps of mud and rotten apples, listening eagerly to the bing bop, bing bop, bing bop noises of our equally imaginary sonar. (Barry insisted we had sonar on our Island, apparently it added to the atmosphere of it all).

And so all was well until something unforetold happened, something that even the biggest brains on Bridge Tree Island had failed to envisage, something so catastrophic that it caused squabbles and lots of harsh words amongst us Cecs of 'What are we going to do now?' Why didn't we make contingency plans ? We could all die of hunger?' and 'Mum's gonna kill me if I don't make it home tonight alive'.

It rained, it poured down, when it didn't stop raining it rained again. Our den got washed away, the mud beneath our feet turned to a pond with bits of mud in it, but worse than that, much worse than that, the trees got wet.

Our only means of getting off Bridge Tree Island was now looking like a firemans pole with cold running water coursing down its entire length, climbing up it would be akin to climbing up a waterfall.

Instantly we all looked at Buzzy, Buzzy was the one, Buzzy's prowess in climbing trees was legendary, Buzzy could out height any one of us, surely he could climb the tree and summon help.

His third attempt got him at least a foot higher than his first two, soaked to the skin he slipped down onto his arse and said something that was for us Cecs only.

We were all doomed to a watery death with Davy Jones's locker having nothing to do with it.

'It will stop raining soon,' Buzzy said, shaking his head and spraying everyone with thick droplets of rainwater from his curly ginger hair.

'Got to stop soon' Mark intoned and managed to intone with no conviction at all.

Les announced that it was getting dark and we all then realised that it was getting dark, things were beginning to get worrying and to add to the misery the water level was showing signs of rising.

I don't remember who suggested it but to us already drenched Cecs it made a modicum of sense.

The main part of the divided river flowed heavily under the bigger of the two arches on our right, maybe the water to our left flowing under the left arch was shallower, it was certainly much narrower. What did we have to lose? We were all completely soaked anyway.

I took my shoes and socks off and put a tentative foot into the water.

'Have another go at climbing the tree Buzzy' I said, my teeth already chattering and my attempts of getting a laugh falling on deaf ears.

The eyes of the world were on me, I took a further step and found the river bed about 10 inches down, rough stones covered with strands of weed and the cold waters freezing my calf muscles. With my arms outstretched for balance I took another two steps and immediately sunk up to my waist in the icy waters. The far bank looked closer but the water between me and it looked black with shark fins cutting large 'V's in its choppy surface. That's one small step for man, one giant leap for all on Bridge Tree Island.

It was time to close my eyes and go for it, I closed my eyes and went for it all balance gone just forward propulsion. The water splashed up onto my face but my feet never lost the river bed and after a couple more frantic steps I reached land and clambered up through the stalks of reeds to claim it.

'Come on in the water's lovely' I shouted to the still stranded, I couldn't keep the smugness out of my voice.

*

Sara and Hoppity

We could achieve huge distances but our targets were perfectly safe, it was totally impossible to attain any reasonable accuracy or indeed control any outcome.

Clay Wangers, (they were a Cecs thing). Let me attempt to relay to you the immense pleasure me Barry, Buzzy and a whole host of other reprobates got from our Clay Wangers.

Firstly a long thin, springy length of willow was selected from the surrounding trees, then from the floor and walls of the clay pits small wodges of said clay were gouged out and rolled in the hand into small rounded balls. These gooey globes were then compressed onto the very thin tips of our Wangers. By holding the thicker end of the Wanger and raising (carefully so your wodge doesn't fall off) you were ready to flick the wanger as hard and as fast over as you could skywards.

After a lot of practice and a few backfires it was possible to snatch your hand downwards at the precise moment and send your wodge of clay hurtling into the lower atmosphere with absolutely no idea where gravity would take over and bring it back to earth.

Clay Wanging…what fun?

*

Space Patrol

Reading West railway station was a lot smaller and less busy than Reading General, it had a long largely empty platforms, and no people in black clothing lurking in the shadows which always meant authority to us Cecs.

You didn't have to pay to go into the station and there were shelters if it rained so, as you can see there was a lot of potential for mischief. A potential we used to its fullest potential.

A carefully placed penny balanced on top of the rail made deliciously flattened shapes when umpteen tons of train wheels went over it, (Note; drill a small hole in it with your dad's black and decker, thread through that hole a length wool and give it to your girlfriend as a magic charm and it could improve your chances of receiving some of her charm later) Mischief…A ball thrown over said train from one platform and caught by a fellow Cec on the platform the other side a feat of amazing dexterity.

Using your clay wanger (see clay wanger) to further decorate the signal lights at the end of the platform with little blobs of wet clay took a certain amount of skill and aim but the real test, the ultimate test was to 'Wheel Watch' called this because you actually 'watched wheels'.

The platform was built on what could only be described as stilts, upright single lined brick built sections that supported the platform itself. Between these uprights was just enough space for a Cec to squeeze in amongst discarded beer cans, newspapers, slow worms (most slow worms go in for train spotting) and colonies of ants and spiders.
This is where we boys would take it in turns to huddle under for the duration of the umpteen ton train to pay a visit to Reading West Railway Station. It was a dare of course, to ascertain how brave you were or how wide your yellow streak was.

Of course you never knew whether the train you got was a 'goer' or a 'stopper', no-one could be bothered to consult the timetable because that would somehow diminish the excitement, the anxiety, not to mention the fact that it would show to others how terrified you really were.
You got what you got, but every Cec prayed for a 'stopper' for their *'turn'*.
A 'stopper' was comparatively easy, you simply climbed down under the platform, screwed yourself into as tight a ball as possible and waited for the inescapable to occur.
Soon, very soon an ear splitting crescendo under the belly of the train came to rest beside you, its shadows ominous, its breaking silver wheels screeching inches from your face.

You lay there unable to move and once the'stopper's' wheels had come to a complete standstill the waiting was agonising.

What if the train had broken down? What if it was due to stop there for hours?

What if the driver had had a heart attack and fallen against the go button and he was fat and they couldn't move him? What if…

And then a clunking noise and with a huge sigh of relief you notice the big silver wheel in your face start moving, ponderously slow but moving.

The shadows are chased away along the length of the underside of the platform by the emerging light and at last you can move your legs and scamper up from your could've been last resting place,

It was now my turn and guess what?

The platform is eerily quiet and calm, the 'stopper' having left a good while ago. The chances of me getting a 'goer' heightened because of it, stood to reason really didn't it ? One after the other.

Was I hearing things or was that the sound of the birds not singing?

Had the trees ceased their gentle swaying or were they just resting?

Was the air really being sucked away upline by the slipstream of the rapidly approaching train?

Was I soon to be decapitated by the 11.15 Great Western Service to Paddington?

The train cometh, the earth (platform) shook beneath my feet in anticipation and Les broke off a bit of his Bar Six and gave it to me, the condemned man's last meal!!

I jumped down onto the rails (or was I pushed?) I lowered my head, got to my knees and crablike made my way under the platform's surface and from somewhere in the far too near distance the sound of a train's angry whistle came to my ears.

I was under the platform in the shadows looking at the rails that were far too big and far too near vibrating with the spread of the huge weight that was about to assault them.

The sudden and unexpected silence meant the train's approach would suddenly become its arrival and there was absolutely nothing I could do about it..

And then It was upon me, the silence now a chaos of rushing air currents and earth moving rumblings, in front of my rapidly blinking eyes the intermediate flash of silver and black as the wheels a blur of indistinct motion left images of whirling confusion burnt into my retinas.

And then the cracks appeared, long deep cracks spreading across the underside of the platform as I looked up in abject terror and through dust-covered eyelashes the cracks became wider and holes appeared between them, large cavernous holes.

Soon I would be buried under tons of ex platform concrete, my own tomb.

It was with gaining confidence that I crawled over to the light from the space in the platform wall and willed myself to put my head out through it.
The fleeting train was now a vanishing blur with all its sounds and motions chasing behind it.
The platform was still standing, the cracks and holes already back in place already for the next few hundred tons of metal to visit it again,
And I was relieved that I didn't have to grasp at muck covered wood and metal supports to stay where I wanted to stay.

Along with an instant laying of light and a deafening silence I heard a voice that all of a sudden occupied my whole being..
'Come on then Buzzy, your turn'

*

'Five and seven eighths inches long, it must be a world record, blimey I ain't seen one bigger' It was Barry looking down in awe at the freshly caught Great Crested Newt. I was holding it carefully by the very end of its tail and had a finger gently on its head, not at all stretching it of course, just attempting to ignore its frantic wriggling. Barry was holding my wooden school ruler against its squirming body.
'Yep' he said, 'Definitely six inches long…at least'.

'This surely should be a record' Barry exclaimed.
'A world record' I exclaimed, but louder.
'How do we get it recorded?'
A silence came over us as we pondered this perplexing question, Barry fondling our potential claim to fame, letting it squirm freely between his fingers, me considering the idea of tying one of my sisters wooden cotton reels to its tail and therefore stretching it further by letting the newt drag it about with it as it waddled along all day.
'The museum' I shouted, waking myself from my own reverie.
'That's what we'll do, take it to Reading (downtown....) museum, bound to be someone clever and who will know what to do.
And that's what we did.
Have you ever tried tying a cotton reel to a newts tail? Can't be done.

Dear reader, I would like to say at this juncture that newts in my day were ten a penny, the lovely little amphibians were plentiful in ponds and lakes everywhere. I realise today they are an endangered species. I would like to think that we made little or no effect on their numbers all those years ago but I admit that probably isn't the case. I apologise to the newt community and I'm very glad today they are now a protected species.

*

The Woodentops

We had never thought to name any of our newts or frogs, too numerous, too much bother but we had to name our would be, could be, on the five o'clock news in the near future Great Crested Newt.
On the bus into Reading, our longest newt specimen safely housed in one of my mums tupperware boxes, we put the time into naming it.
After a good number of bus stops and a good number of silly names we finally agreed on a name that was fitting for a newt of this magnitude....Newton.
Arriving in Reading we quickly made our way to the huge imposing building next to the Town Hall that housed the museum.
We each had visited the museum on many occasions, sometimes to peruse the wonderful artefacts it displayed but mostly to meet girls, it being free to enter, quiet and having many secluded sections.
'Can we see the man in charge please?'
Barry was talking to a man dressed like an important man.
'How can I help you young men'
I don't know how the others felt but being called 'young man' from then on I was going to sound all my aitches and not say bloody once.

Barry held up the tupperware box, lifted its lid and told the important looking man that we thought Newton was probably the longest newt in the world. The important looking man peered into the box and said that he thought it could easily be the biggest newt in the world and he would put it in his book, take our names and would we be good young men and take it back to the pond where we got it from as such a big newt would need to go back so it could grow even bigger and thank you very much for bringing it in to show him but didn't we think newts should be left where they live, thank you very much, and was gone.
Barry told him it was called Newton and we went to get the bus home.

*

We'd often go 'Newting', it was being out with nature at its best, we all did it, us Cecs. No need for girlie things like nets, us boys would balance on outcrops of rocks or bits of half submerged wood over deep pools of frog and newt infested waters and use our bare hands to scoop them up.
Concentration that was the name of the game, concentration and the reflexes of striking cobra. Splash, 'oh Christ another 'wet one' was often the only sounds heard for hours. Another 'wet one' was our terminology for a wellington boot full of freezing

cold pond water as a result of a fellow Cec slipping off his observation point and to avoid falling in completely having to stick his entire leg into the possibly cholera infected water.

Many a time I've sat wringing a sock out only to soak my other sock minutes later. It was the price you paid to 'newt', the price you paid to spend time with fellow Cecs and paddle for a while in *their* lives.

'I'll have the old one for growing onions in' Mrs Haines told the Council worker as he hefted the 'old one' out ready to put it in the skip.

The 'old one' was her kitchen sink. Made of thick white china it was the size of a small swimming pool and weighed half a ton. They were used by us Cecs mothers all over the estate for washing up in, washing clothes in, peeling spuds in and on cold winter mornings washing us in. Saved wasting hot water filling the bath.

However this particular defunct kitchen sink never got to see a single onion; instead it was the perfect container to house our large and growing collection of newts and frogs. Until of course the old Copper boiler came to replace it (but more of that later). Solid walls, open top, slippery surfaces (prison walls should be made of it) and a plug hole in the bottom for easy cleaning and de-mudding.

And so it was that our amphibian zoo was complete, inhabited by happy well looked after newts, furnished with clods of mud, rocks and clumps of grass, it was the place we spent many fulfilling hours, Johnny Morrising around.

*

Pinky and Perky

A Copper Boiler was usually made of galvanised steel, cylindrical in shape with a circular lid. It was used for heating water to wash clothes and a tap at its base to drain the water from after. I can still see my mum filling it with buckets of water and stirring the clothes with a bleached white stick.

'It's a twin tub'
For some reason (totally alien to me) mum was excited about her new washing machine. I was more interested in the big wooden tweezer-like thing that came with it, it would be great for picking up newts and frogs as long as you were careful not to squeeze too hard and squash them.

Dad was huffing and puffing carrying the old copper boiler out of the back door to put it in the back garden for storing, storing what I had no idea but as a new home for our frogs and newts it would be perfect.
Frogs being frogs had a tendency to hop out of the old sink, it being too low sided, too many of them escaped and hopped it.
The newts envious of the frogs but unable to hop, would tie lengths of grass together and abseil to freedom (in my imagination) of course but even so a lot of them managed a Colditz.
The copper being much taller on the sides would prove to be just the job and do just the job, we could even leave the lid up so the inhabitants could get some air.
Barry, Mark and I made the amphibians feel more at home by putting the requisite bits in the bottom i.e. Grass sods, stones and worms and I swear I saw a few of them smile when we placed them inside, but it wasn't long before tragedy struck, the next morning actually.
Although we didn't keep exact records of individual numbers (too boring) it was clearly evident that our cooper was a few newts and frogs lighter. Slimy trails and drips of water lining the insides of the copper led us to the awful conclusion that some of the more determined creatures had effected a successful escape and more than likely were now lining the

stomachs of the local Council Estate Gulls, Pigeons, crows and no doubt cats.

A remedy to this catastrophe had to be sought, and no time wasted in the soughting. Vaseline jelly,(I think it was Mark's idea) a thin layer of vaseline borrowed from the bathroom cabinet and smeared along the underside of the top of the copper should do the trick. And that's what we did, all we had to do now was wait and watch.

Encouraged obviously by observing their fellow captees all night through it wasn't long before the braver of the newts started to scale the copper's sheer vertical sides. 'They'll get as far as the vaseline and slip back down' Mark whispered excitedly in my ear as the three of us stood mesmerised by the sights unfolding before us.

It turned out to be a resounding flop.

As the newts entered the vaseline zone the three of us exhaled huge gasps of disbelieve, not one of the newts even looked like slipping back, in fact the gooey vaseline having had time to clog assisted in the newts endeavours and I'm convinced some of them even accelerated to the top.

So it was put the lid down overnight or find another method to keep the captives captive. Barry suggested tin foil, I suggested barbed wire and look out post with big lights and armed guards…suggestions that resulted in a lot of rolling

about laughing and even more creative suggestions.
We put the lid down at night from then on.

*

The flat piece of slate was quite big and hurt my
fingertips as I gently raised it. Steve stood by waiting
to snatch one if he saw one.
'Yes' he shouted excitedly 'And quite a big one'.
Slow worms were fascinating to us boys, we knew
they were not snakes but legless lizards but we liked
to catch them. Slow worms had pitch black protruding
eyes and round shiny heads with funny little smiley
mouths, they couldn't bite and seemed quite friendly.
Snakes we were very careful to avoid. The adder had
a pointed head, flicking tongue, black warning zig
zag's down its back and a bitey face with a long
flicking tongue and looked the business.
Yes, we avoided snakes at all costs. Except of
course when we were poking them with a stick
encouraging them to coil and strike. Apart from that
we largely left them alone.

*

Windy Miller

It was an old clay mine building smelling of oil and
grease, it was standing tall on top of a dead end road

almost totally obscured by dense bushes and trees. Although on route to our school, Stoneham Secondary Modern we never paid it or the area much attention, but on this particular Saturday for reasons now forgotten it became the focus of ours.
Between the bushes running from the buildings opened doors to the road that seemed a hundred miles the rails ran over a large hump in the earth and further down to a rusty and rickety set of buffers.
It didn't take a genius to work out that these rails were once used to transport clay and equipment up and down the reasonably steep incline.

'What if ?' Someone in our little gang of would be vandals said..'What if we could get that wagon thingy moving we could…?' he didn't need to say another word, the images of said wagon hurtling down the incline at breakneck speed were instantly the only thing that mattered in the minds of nine (socks round their ankles, holes in their jumpers, delinquent boys). A cloud of dried sand and brick dust followed us into the shadows of the brickhouse and in seconds 18 skinny arms and 18 spindly legs were put to good use in pushing the wagon back out into the sunshine it hadn't seen for a good few years.
After protesting its reluctance for an annoying length of time and causing the hasty retreat of a thousands of spiders and the destruction of their webs the

wagon started to slowly move, its wheels crying out with metal arthritis.

We finally had it out of the brickhouse and sitting in all its glory on the sand covered rails, it was only then that we realised that said rails had a tendency to disappear under said sand and said wheels would soon become sunk if said wagon was pushed any further. We would need to remove said sand from said rails before said wagon went anywhere.

So after a round of fruit gums (I was always wary about ending up with a green one) and armed with branches and sticks torn from the surrounding bushes we set to work clearing the rails.

The work was hot but the enthusiasm was hotter, in no time at all we had the rails clear and (Thunderbird 2, Michael's idea I think) ready for her maiden shove and shove we did.

Eight near skeletal bare chested kids with the spirit of Isambard Kingdom Brunel coursing through our veins we managed to get her out from the shadow of the shed.

From there we only had to get to the top of the flat terrain where the rails were almost level on the ground beneath it and a few more steps further until we reached the beginning of the incline and allowed gravity to take over.

And then almost imperceptibly it did, Thunderbird 2 was gradually gaining speed, picking up momentum, becoming a force of its own, looking back at us every now and again and tipping us the wink...

It wasn't until Thunder 2 had started to accelerate and we found that running alongside screaming and laughing was becoming more of a race that she was winning, the more astute of us began to wonder how the hell we were going to stop it.

Below, and beyond the hump the buffers, which now looked to us as if a puff of wind could easily take them away, was the road, a busy road with cars and pedestrians, a road that according to us excited boys just *wasn't really there before.*

With Thunderbird 2 now showing us a clean pair of a set of four steel wheels and with a following cloud of sandy dust in its wake we could do no more than sink to our knees and watch, fighting the almost overwhelming urge to run in the opposite direction.

It hit the hump, rose slightly in the air and unlike the real Thunderbird 2 did not stay in it. I remember having a glimmer of hope that it would derail itself soon and land on its side its wheels sinking into the sand

causing it to jolt to a stop.

Some of us looked elsewhere searching desperately for something far more interesting to look at, some of us buried our heads in our hands and prayed, some of us were totally incapable of doing either and just stared opened mouthed.

Tons of Thunderbird 2 was now travelling at warp factor 7, either it was getting closer to the road (which now had everybody that lived on the estate and their uncles on it) or the road was getting closer to it.

One hope, one forlorn hope…the buffers.

And that's when everything went into slow motion mode...or to put it another way, when the shit hit the fan.

Thunderbird 2, hit the buffers, and in an instant its rear wheels left the rails and its back end rose into the air

A millisecond later the sound of splintering wood and twisting metal bouncing over an iron cattle grid met our ears and a cloud of sand and dirt obscured the whole dramatic scene from our eyes.

In an instant a deafening silence surrounded us kids, the birds stopped chirping, the traffic noise ceased and the trees around us stopped growing.

We stood mesmerised as the demise of Thunderbird 2 was slowly revealed to our searching eyes.

She was standing upright amongst the buffers, on her front end in a mess of tangled wood and metal wreckage and just like in all the best car crash films, the sun was glinting off one of her rear wheels that was still spinning.

*

Mr Benn

'Lets try the Precinct, there's always plenty of people up there shopping and Sandra can push it in the pushchair'
My sister glared at me.
'Why me, why can't Serena or Jackie push it?'
'Take it in turns then, it's a girly thing' (chauvinism hadn't been invented yet).
Sometimes it felt like I had fifty sisters.
Bob grinned as he pretended to fix a wheel on the pushchair that didn't need fixing, he tilted it up by its axle and Guy Faulks head fell off again and rolled towards the road.
'Oops'
Nobody laughed, nobody felt like laughing, the Medway Precinct was virtually uphill all the way.
'Why do we have to go all the way up there?'
It was Sandra moaning again.
'Because there are far more people there and people means money'
Our Guy wasn't very heavy and he looked more like a guyess as his face was painted on by my female siblings using their cheap and garish Woolies bought makeup.
With an old grey nightshirt shirt of Mrs Haines (donated without her consent) and stuffed with old copies of the Daily Mirror and the News of the World

he at least looked well fed. When his head wasn't on the ground he wore a black velvet hat on it mum wasn't missing yet (no funerals on the horizon) and for trousers a pair of Bob's pyjama bottoms covered over by dad's old painter and decorators dungarees. The Guy wasn't expected to walk anywhere so we put slippers on a pair of stuffed socks and sellotaped the whole ensemble to the bottom of his legs.

As long as the fishing line (my idea as you could barely see it) held, our Guy who would sit and not slouch.

We set off passing around a packet of (stuck in my pocket for days and sticky) Old English flavour Spangles. We must have looked a strange sight, striding up Honey End Lane pushing a pushchair with a six foot baby sitting in it dragging its knuckles along the pavement and every now and then having to stop to put its head back on.

Standing outside the 'Bookies' (Dad's influence on me even then, you're far more likely to get money from a gambler who has won on the gee gees especially if they've had a drink as well) we'd put on our politest voices and say 'Penny' for the Guy' Most people gave us money without even looking at our guy which suited us Cecs because it was a rubbishy Guy anyway.

*

It probably started as early as October, *Firework Night,* or at least when the fireworks started to appear in the shops. Standard, Pains, Astra, Black Cat, fireworks, namely… Roman Candles, Silver Fountains, Catherine Wheels, Jumping Jacks, Bangers (easily us boys favourites) Brocks Bombshell Repeaters,Traffic Lights, Golden Rain, Rebel Raisers, Snow Fountains, Rising Sun, Ariel Shell Sparklers…etc,etc..

V

(I've left the space for you to list your own favourites) and of course all manner of Rockets, from mini hand launched Rockets to Rockets fired from empty milk bottles taped to fence poles and Nuclear Rockets that screamed into the air lighting up the entire sky and burning out your retinas then plunging back to earth to dent the bonnet of an unfortunate car owners car. With very little respect to pet owners, us Cecs would fire off fireworks at the flick of a match (on behalf of my fellow Cecs, my belated and useless apologies to our neighbours).

We called them Genies...hoping not to sound too much like a pyromaniac we would get a few bangers, break them in half and pour their black contents (gun powder) onto a flat surface making a little pile.

When a naked flame was introduced to the little pile it would instantly become an exploding supernova and if you were standing too close your eyelashes and eyebrows would disappear leaving an acrid singed hair aroma to follow you the rest of the day.
Another favourite would be to pull the rubber grips of your bike's handlebars, light the bangers blue fuse, wait for the warning fizz, shove the angry banger into the hollow handlebars, push the rubber grip back, stand away and put your dirty fingers in your dirty ears and watch the grip fly through the air followed by a cannon's blast of smoke.

*

Bagpuss

The challenge was to light your banger from the pilot light in the gas water heater (Ascot) on the wall in the kitchen, wait for the end to start fizzing (little sparks flying from them, like the sticks of dynamite in the best westerns) then run like hell (you've got about 10 seconds) through the kitchen to the back door and once in the back garden throw the banger skyward. Success meant watching your banger spinning in the air and then hearing the bang as your banger banged. Failure to get out of the kitchen quick enough meant possibly burnt fingers, blackened cheekbones, singed hair and a ringing in your ears that lasted all day.

Oh yeah, and a kitchen smelling like rotten eggs.

*

'I can see someone moving about but it's too dark to see what they are doing'. Sandra had the curtain pulled back slightly and her open hand pressed to the glass to cover any glare from the lights inside the room. Peering out into the back gardens she kept turning back to us kids to keep us informed of what was happening, she'd been doing that for the best part of an hour.

We'd sat and watched the map of the Ponderosa burn from the centre to its extremes on Bonanza and soon it would be our turn to 'bring forth the flame'. It was bonfire night, the 5th of November, an historic night for England and a highly enjoyable time for us Cecs on the Southcote Estate to boot.

All through the proceeding weeks single rockets would now and again illuminate the sky and bangers made their presence felt by exploding in random places but the actual night that was bonfire night began with a building tension, a growing anticipation and a pregnant lull that lay across the land until the first fires and fireworks were lit and then culmination of the lunacy was widespread, all the time spreading wider.

Outside and into the darkening (fireworkless for now sky) Bob and I had jumped over the fence and made our way (SAS like) through the long grass and stinging nettles of the backfields.

Our mission was to find out if any of our neighbours had succumbed and lit their back garden bonfires yet or set off any fireworks. Why set fire to the huge pile of wood, cardboard and paper you had painstakingly gathered for weeks prior to this night and miss everybody else whilst enjoying yours. Someone always lit theirs first, it had to be; the trick was to be there when they did.

Serena, the thinker of the family had it sussed, 'The Davies's would light theirs first, they've got young kids, but the fireworks they let off would be the type that hissed and just farted, 'well you can't have everything' Sandra would reply.

And then the cry would go out...'The Haines have lit theirs' and in a flurry of stampeding kids everyone made their way to their garden to see the three inch flames that had just begun to flourish and the promise they held.

Soon the inevitable temptation would win through, other fires were lit, smoke began to billow into the sky obliterating the stars, choruses of oohs and ahhs filled the air and pre-prepared tin foil wrapped

potatoes thrown into the blossoming infernos, bottles of corona opened and the show starter sparklers lit).
As the smoke became more dense and the sound of laughter and shouts of excitement merged with it I realise now in hindsight that we ourselves were caught up in the moment, in the together, the Cecs of Southcote Estate.
But now our young eyes begin to sting and our lungs turn into smoke filled balloons.
Years later a lovely old friend gave me her recollections. It was good to hear.
Bonfire nights when the air was full of smoke from so many back garden bonfires and that smell of fireworks as we stood in the damp air writing our names with the sparklers. Rockets launched from milk bottles (who even gave it a second thought how potentially dangerous that could be?)
As I say Firework night on the Southcote Estate was always a monumental affair for the getting together of so many (and the filling of the wards of the local A&E a testament to that fact).

*

It's now called the Medway Precinct, a large shopping Centre in Tilehurst. It used to be a clay pit, a very big clay pit with high sand and clay walls and a deep

pond in its middle. The clay was thick and rich, ideal for wanging clay, which no doubt was the very origin of the clay wanger.
Us Cecs spent many an hour climbing the seriously steep and sometimes crumbling walls in the knowledge that a fall would only result in a landing in a bramble bush, sand or soggy clay.
My brother Bob had found an old rusted penknife, I wanted it.
'Ok' he said, 'You can have it if you do a dare' My elder brother being four years older than me got great pleasure in teasing and tormenting me. All elder brothers in those days were bullies - Bob was no exception.

'Bet you can't get to Coronation Square and get me some fags in under ten minutes. I was off like a shot..'Well how did I do?'... 'What..Oh 9 mins well done' He was lighting one up as I walked away..

We were standing at the top of one of the walls Bob and I and below us the sand had obviously been blown up against the side of said wall making a sort of leaning sand dune against it, the bottom of which was about fifteen feet underneath us. Bob opened the knife and threw it down where it landed with a soft thud onto the top of the mound of sand.
'Jump down and get it and it's yours' he said licking his lips and then spitting down after it.

I stood as if I were standing on top of Mount Kilimanjaro staring down at a speck of rust half buried in the soft sand. Three maybe four times I stepped towards the mountain's edge each time I hesitated and stepped back.

The fifth time I jumped. I hit the sand, toppled over forwards and rolled down towards the firmer surface of clay with the pen knife stuck in my left buttock.

Tom Brown took me to the hospital where I had three stitches, a tetanus jab and the pen knife confiscated.

*

Torchy the Battery Boy

French Arrows…no idea why we called them French Arrows but it was the name they went by. Much like Clay Wanger's, French arrows had to be long, thin in shape but more importantly completely smooth (If you had been given enough pocket money or your dad was drunk, as was more likely in my case, you could buy real arrows from a hobby shop). We would often buy the dyed green sticks sold in garden centres for plant props.

One end of the stick was sharpened to a point, which in hindsight probably made it a lethal and therefore an illegal weapon, the other end was split and fitted with a handmade paper flight.

Thin twine was now needed, again as smooth as possible and about 2ft long. A knot was tied as tightly as we could manage about an inch from the end of said twine.

Now the knotted part of the twine was looped ONCE around the arrow at the flight end and held it in place around the knot..
Holding the arrow at its sharpened tip between thumb and forefinger, the slack in the twine from the flight end was taken up. Making sure the knot was not disturbed or moved from its position just below the flight take off was imminent.
Pinching the arrow tip and twine together the arrow was ready to be sent skyward using an overhead spear throwing motion.
Just before the arrow was clear of the twine, a sudden downward jerk of the wrist (if timed perfectly) would give the arrow incredible forward thrust)
With luck and practise the arrow flew great distances and embedded itself in a tree or in the ground..With bad luck it would fly a great distance and embed itself in someone's chest.
Please Do NOT try this at home!

*

Coronation Square. It wasn't a square at all; it was a large area of grass with rounded ends and a square middle, all surrounded by a road, not unlike a speedway track. In the summer, fetes and sometimes fun fairs were held on it.

On one side of this 'square' and across the road were a row of shops,(collectively known to us locals as 'Corries') a Library, a fish and chip shop, a barbers (where all us school kids got the identical haircuts despite what we asked for, a short back and sides) a betting office (an essential commodity in those days) a chemist, a hardware store, a newsagents/sweetshop a fruit and veg shop, a post office and an off-licence.

In front of the shops and before the road were long low brick and concrete structures (we called them bunkers for some obscure reason) They were used for sitting on, resting bikes against, anchoring dogs to and anything else you could use a long low brick and concrete structure for.

We Cecs were convinced they were full of hidden Gestapo bodies from the war.

One fateful day I used them to discover what it meant to be a boy and to pay particular care and attention to my testicals.

At one end of these brick structures stood a bright red and wet (because it had recently rained, letter box).

I will let my mate Les relate the rest of this story because even after all these years I still find the telling of it far too painful.(I'm sure many of you have already guessed the gist of my tale of woe but please keep it to yourselves).

Anyway, here goes…

I cannot remember who it was, it might have been Barry or Les, but someone bet Kim he wouldn't run along the top of the bunker and leapfrog over the letter box (the bet was a whole packet of fruit pastilles if I remember correctly)…I was about to remind Kim about the letter box being wet but he had already started his run. I watched Kim as he gained speed along the top of the bunker, I watched as he reached the end and began his short journey through the air, I watched as he parted his legs and placed both hands on top of the letter box, I watched as half of the letter box disappeared under his crotch, I watched as both of his hands slipped off the letterboxes top…I had to stop watching.

*

'Where are we going to meet for your birthday?'
Her name was Laura and she was tiny.
How about Corries? ' I replied, digging in my pockets for my chewing gum.
'What time?'

'Oh, seven or eight, depending when football finishes'
I replied.

Five to eight.

She walked across the green towards us, Barry and I.
She wore a pure white dress and looked like she had
just fallen from a Christmas tree.
Barry and I burst into fits of laughter.
Laura, wherever you are now, I am so truly sorry.

Trumpton

Staying for a while in Coronation Square, it was also
home to a Youth Club, a club where kids could get
together and swear, talk and spit away from the
prying ears and eyes of interfering adults, a place
where furtive kisses were ok as long as you were
both standing up whilst performing them, a place for
cool cats like us.
The club was called the 'Cool Cat Club' and it was
there that I learned to smoke a cigarette and chew
gum at the same time with panache and
nonchalance.
A vague guide to the cigarettes individual Cool Cats
smoked could say a lot about the smokee from my
own observations.

Sovereign, Players No.6, or No.10, Corsair, and roll ups, Gold Virginia, Old Holburn' you were from the ravaged part of the Estate, the part where at least one parent was out of work or incarcerated. Embassy, Embassy Regal, Benson and Hedges, Silk Cut, Woodbine, Weights, a part of the estate where both parents had employment. Rothmans, Marlborough, Piccadilly, both parents worked and you had a part time job helping the milkman on his rounds, Peter Styvescent, Gauloises, you stole them, Craven A, and Capstan, you had a death wish, Consulate and Everest you were probably gay.

Of course our club in Southcote was a magnet for our bitter rivals from nearby Tilehurst and Coley. Many skirmishes were carried out within the walls of the Cool Cat club, sometimes spilling out onto the grassy area of Coronation square, fists flying and back pushing to the music blaring out from the jukebox in the hall. A good few eyes were blackened to the rhythm of *'I can see clearly now, the rain has gone'* and shins bruised to the lyrics of *'Summer's here and the time is right, for dancing in the street'* not to mention rivers of tears fallen from the words of *'The world is just a great big onion'..* Music, the food of life. Coronation Square was so busy during those early years.

*

Friday night disco night at the Cool Cat Club..be there or be square..no way did I want to be square. The music filling my ears, the ice cold pepsi on occasion filling my nose as I bopped up and down with Carol, Ann, Jean and Sara probably not looking so cool. When not bopping up and down I would stand by the speakers near the DJ's decks watching the action and getting some of my cool back.

She was beautiful, her ponytails catching the flashing lights, the top three buttons of her cardigan undone and she was walking towards me ignoring all my fellow cool catters.

At last someone with taste. Our eyes met as the Walker Brothers were suggesting that the sun wasn't gonna shine anymore. She looked up at me through her N.H.S. glasses and spoke to me through her teeth braces..'Do you have Dynamic Pressure ?' Wow, what a chat up line ?. How was I to know that she thought I was with the disco and Dynamic Pressure was the latest record by Boris Gardiner...I kept that one to myself.

*

Watch with Mother

Adjacent to the Cool Cat Club stood a smaller building, mum often sent me there to pick up big tins of SMA and Cow and Gate milk, a sort of clinic I think ..but the building itself had a far greater use as far as us young Council Estate Creations (Cecs) were concerned...Behind this building and away from the prying eyes of adults and patrolling policemen (yes in my day policemen actually got out of their cars) the shadowed corners, ideal for all kinds of things were thusly utilised.

One in particular activity that I am unashamedly proud of, I am more than happy to relate to you.. I held the record for the longest uninterrupted, lips locked together, arms tightly embracing, no giggling snog. Well of course Linda Morgan played her part in it but me being not only the instigator but also the creator of such activity I take all the credit.

With Lynne and Barry Haines as witnesses and watch holders Linda and I had a couple of rehearsals, quickly because neither of us wanted to use up too much of our valuable saliva reserves.

Then the scene was set. Barry started a countdown 10 to one, Linda spat out her chewing gum and leant her back against the brickwall, I blew my nose and stuffed the tissue into the front pocket of my short trousers, (pushing my catapult to oneside) and then we both took great sucks of air into our lungs, did a synchronised puckup of our of lips and.... SMACK.

The first 10 seconds were fine, just a regular snog really, eyes tightly closed so we didn't have to look at each other and burst out laughing.

20 seconds in and we had to blank out the sniggering from the small audience or we ourselves would burst out laughing.

30 seconds in and the 'bends' started to creep into our brains and the wanting to burst out laughing was almost overwhelming.

40 seconds in and the pent up laughter was escaping our tightly meshed lips in little sprayed spittle geysers.

50 seconds in and if Barry hadn't shouted 'Nearly a minute' I swear we would have made it a minute.

Our separation was an eruption in reverse, a pushing apart of epic proportions, Linda tried to turn and embed herself into the bricks of the wall, I fell backwards gasping for breath, the catapult in my pocket snapping and a sharp splinter of it sticking into my inside thigh far too close to certain other bits of my body. As I hit the floor the tears of pain and laughter mingled with the copious amounts of mutually ejected snot already on my face.

Barry looked down at me, handed me the watch and looking at Lynne

said..'Our turn'

*

Chigley

The acoustics were incredible, the sound seemed to travel all around Prospect park, footballers stopped footballing, dog owners stopped for a while owning their dogs, but more important than any of that, the opposite sex became suddenly more aware of us. Between the huge cylindrical concrete pillars holding the protruding bow fronted windows of the mansion's roof up and standing on top of a raised platform us boys strutted our stuff.

My Discatron Discaset freshly fed with new batteries blasted out the sounds of the day which were bounced and amplified from the walls and windows at our backs.

'I can't get no Satisfaction, The Stones, Good vibrations, The Beach Boys, Mama told me not to come, Three Dog Night, In the Summertime, Mungo Jerry and many many more (well as many records we could carry in two carrier bags).

People would stop and stare (Everybody's talkin, Glen Cambell).

We probably had that in one of the bags as well. People near us saw us miming the words to the songs and we (the stars of the show) would take turns to change the records, getting up from our chosen spots on the platform all nonchalantly like puffing on our Number 6s (Rothmans' if we were in the in the money) as if we had far better things to do, after all we were Cool Cats were we not?

When eventually a few girls came up and sat on the end of the platform and started fiddling with their makeup and moving not so discreetly towards the music whilst pretending not to notice us adonis's we realised we had it made, not sure exactly what we had made, but we had made it anyway!

And all was well until the man in the black jacket approached us making tut, tut noises that we could hear even over the sound of The Monkees telling everyone that they were all believers.

'Sorry lads you can't make that noise on these premises, you'll have to move somewhere else'

In those days and at our age you didn't reply with obscenities, you didn't stand and argue or threaten violence, you were much more likely to seek out the offending person's car and wee on its wheels.

Growing no more than 100 ft away from the Mansion House was the 'Monkey Tree', a huge beast that because of its unique shape and ground level branches was popular with us Cecs for lounging in. This tree was an ancient fir and its lower boughs grew so low that the underside of them were actually submerged into the ground, the tops of which were worn glassy smooth by the thousands of bums that had spent time sitting on them.

It was the ideal tree to slouch on and do James Dean postures over without actually having to climb it. Between these lower boughs were numerous deep natural cavities that made excellent storage spaces for our cans of coke, packets of biscuits and crisps and of course our record playing Discatron Discaset and bags of records. So when evicted from the Mansions platform by the jobsworth of the day it was the obvious option to us nomadic Cecs to become our new site of residence.

And to add advantage to disadvantage the girls followed.

*

Egg fried rice, sometimes if you were flush it would be sweet and sour pork with egg fried rice, but as I say that was only when you were flush, on this particular hot evening we were anything but flush, a plastic tub of egg fried rice (from the local 'Chinkee' racism wasn't invented then) eaten with an equally plastic spoon.

We were walking down the Oxford Road miming and strutting to the Stones singing about satisfaction on my Discatron Discasset when Barry noticed the upstairs window of a house was wide open and something glinted in his evil eye.

He filled his plastic spoon full of egg fried rice and flicked it with forefinger and thumb through said open window. After a good ten minutes of raucous laughter we changed the record to 'In the summertime' by Mungo Jerry and soon found another opened bedroom window.

It was finally my turn and my first 'flick' almost missed its target because of my efforts to concentrate while stifling the need to burst out laughing again.

Quite a few more bedroom carpets and dressing tables were adorned with maggot looking grains of rice until we ran out of 'ammo' and made our way home.

Today, being of a sound mind and a sounder sense of proprietary we offer our sincerest apologies to all those who had been 'riced' that momentous evening.

*

The Adventures of Twizzle

'Yoghourt face'(she called me because of my darker skin) but I didn't mind, we were so deeply in love nothing else seemed to matter. I missed football practice, fishing and swimming in the Holy Brook with my fellow Cecs to be with her. I would have given my tortoise, Blodwin, to a family of gipsies (there were

plenty of them around) if she asked me to. I would
stop eating Rollos and eat cabbage, I would miss
entire episodes of 'Lost in Space' , I would hang my
clothes up and change the toilet roll when it needed
it...I was besotted even if I didn't know what the word
besotted meant. I was the envy of the Southcote
Estate Cecs because I was going out with a poshy
She lived in a big posh house in Tilehurst and she
called her old lady, Mummy, but that didn't put me off.
Her name was Sidonie and I would marry her one
day and on that you could bet your best conker.
But the course of true love never did run smooth and
ours was doomed the day when a lot of us arrived at
the Coronation Square Newsagents to collect the
fliers we were to be given £3.00 each to deliver.
'Better take your names' the man behind the counter
said as he pointed to us one at a time…
Barry, Mark, Lesley, Christine, Kim, Sidonie, Sandra,
Kevin, Linda.
'Right' he said as he wrote them down on his
clipboard..
'Be better if you split into pairs, girl with boy, boy with
girl, right..
Mark you go with Sandra, Barry you go with Linda,
Christine you go with Lesley, and Kim you go with
Sid.
We knew then it was going to be hard work, a boy
called Kim going out with a girl called Sid, on the
Southcote Estate, Reading.

But one terrible black day the inevitable thing happened.

'I am moving, Kim, it breaks my heart but daddy has got a new job and we are all moving!'

Well you can imagine how I felt but then I saw a ray of light, love springs eternal and all that.

'Where are you moving to Sid you are not going too far I hope?'

She looked past me at the railway siding, behind the bus terminal, unable to look into my eyes afraid of seeing the pain she was bestowing on me.

'Quincy' was her breathless reply.

Now I was quite a travelled Cec even in those days, Mortimer, Burghfield Common, Calcot, Hayling Island, Bognor Regis.

I put my hands on her shoulders and caught her eyes with mine.

'Quincy, where's Quincy, is it Aldermaston way?'

'Massachusetts' Sid replied. Massachusetts USA, Quincy is in Massachusetts'.

I got the feeling she just liked saying Massachusetts and all I could think of was the Bee Gees singing about how they'd like to go back there.

Well I was devastated and couldn't imagine life without her but a few days later after many fervent goodbyes she was finally gone.

She vowed she would never forget me and we'd get married if she ever returned to England and we wrote to each other almost weekly. It got a bit expensive after a while.

I showed Helen a photo of Sid when we were alone in her bedroom a few weeks later listening to 'Can't help falling in love' by Andy Williams and eating Maltesers from a family size bag and drinking Ice Cream Soda Corona.

Helen said Sid looked tarty.

*

He had a dog called Prince, a big black mongrel that was old and fat.

Keith wandered around the estate making friends with all us Cecs by way of sweets and treats. Mum said he was harmless and no more than a kid himself, which made us laugh because he told me he was 28 and therefore as far as I was concerned nearly dead. Keith lived in a flat along the Bath Road, when you asked him what job he did he always said the same which made me laugh.

'I'm in the movie business' he would say with his face as straight as a wooden school ruler.

He worked for Pickfords, the removal firm, we all knew that.

Keith had a trick involving Prince that at first had us Cecs in awe.

Keith would say to Prince..'What is three plus two?'
and Prince would stare up at us and slowly bark out
five times.
'Prince what is 2 + 2 ?'
Bark, bark, bark, bark'
Until Beverly noticed the sore spot on Prince's neck
under his chain collar and saw Keith tug on it the
required number of times we all thought Prince was a
very clever dog, not an exploited one.
Keith took us swimming and bought me a new fishing
rod.
Keith was generous to a fault, until we realised we
were the faults.

*

HuckleBerry Hound Show

We'd circled them enough times looking in their
direction with the hope they would look back in ours
at least once, *(did they just then or were we
hallucinating?)* They were standing by the drinking
water pedestal and didn't seem to be in any hurry to
leave, a good sign surely?

Sorry dear reader but I need to get something off my chest at this juncture. I will resume with my girl meets boy saga later..

Not only did they exist but you could find them almost everywhere. Drinking fountains. Every schoolyard had one, bus and railway stations had one and Prospect Park had one.
The one in the park was Victorian built, it stood 3ft high on a concrete plinth and by pressing a little tap it dribbled water into a metal bowl.
The drinker would bend down press said tap and placing his mouth over the tap, partake of tepid water and unquestionably countless germs from countless other previous drinkers. Who needed a plague to kill them or make them sick when all you had to do was to treat yourself to a drop of water from the nearest drinking fountain.
I digress..

Walking towards girls always resulted in them walking or running away from Les and I but on this occasion unless they were waiting for their boyfriends to turn up, they didn't move.
Nope, they didn't move, they were chatting to each other with no sign of any blind dogs around or white sticks leaning against the water fountain they didn't look overly alarmed at the sight of us with our long

hair, cheesecloth shirts, patched flared jeans, earrings and bus drivers black trench coats.
Council Estate meets private estate, it was a revelation to both sexes and a lot of fun while it lasted.
But was this the beginning of the end?. Had these lovely lasses from the other side of the fence helped in the slow process of taking the Council from the Creation?
Still, after all these years' I cannot pass a stretch of water without scanning the banks in the hope of finding a suitably shaped stone for a 'dead man's fart' or fight the urge to go swimming in a river. I hanker over using a catapult, a claywanger, playing marbles, being obnoxious, or climbing up the side of an old barn. Watching a firework display from a distance just doesn't do it for me, I want to walk through the smoke and get down and dirty.
I don't do any of these things anymore..but I miss them.

Judy and Christine were to be long term girlfriends of ours and in later years Les and Christine became engaged, they didn't eventually marry but that is their story not mine. Judy and I were content to sit in an old semi hollow tree in Prospect Park and while the hours away listening to Tony Blackburn and watching the world go by before gradually drifting apart.

*

Picture Book..

(and for those who have read it, I sincerely hope 'I'm a Council Estate Creation' has indeed been…A Picture